CASTING THE BONES

An Author's Guide
to the
Craft of Fiction

ROBERT GREGORY BROWNE

BRAUN HAUS MEDIA, LLC

TABLE OF CONTENTS

Most of the story examples I've used in this book come from movies, even when those movies were based on books.

Why?

Because many of us have seen the same movies, but not a lot of us have read the same books. So, I've generally used movies that have been around for awhile:

Gone With the Wind
To Kill a Mockingbird
The Godfather
Romancing the Stone
The Fugitive
The Sum of All Fears
Resurrection
Die Hard With a Vengeance

I chose these movies because they are easily accessible to most people, and most of us already know the basic characters and storylines.

When it comes down to it, however, none of the points made really require viewing of any of these movies. They are provided merely as reference points to help clarify the ideas presented.

WHO IS THIS GUY?

And Why Should I Trust Him?

I don't blame you for wondering.

I have a nice little fan base for my fiction, but there are a lot of you who have absolutely no idea who I am, or why I think I'm qualified to write a guide on the craft of fiction.

So where do I start?

I could bore you with the story of wanting to be a writer since I was thirteen years old. How I knew the moment I read Donald Westlake's *Somebody Owes Me Money* that I wanted to be able to do what he'd done.

I could get into my detour into television and screenwriting that landed me a deal with Showtime, and the years I spent writing *Spider-Man* cartoons and other animated shows.

But I won't waste your time with all of that.

What I'll tell you instead is that I'm a veteran writer who has been plying my trade for nearly thirty years, and have published multiple books under various names with St. Martin's Press, Penguin/Dutton, and Harlequin Intrigue.

I've written comedy, thrillers, supernatural, mystery and, yes, romance. My first novel, *Kiss Her Goodbye*, was bought and produced for CBS Television by the people who created *Justified* and *Elementary* (and starred Dylan Walsh, of *Nip/Tuck* fame), and my story, *Bottom Deal*, was also optioned for production by Future Frame.

I've had short stories published in *EasyRider* magazine and in the anthologies *Killer Year*, edited by Lee Child, and *Thriller 3: Love is Murder*, edited by Sandra Brown.

Since 2012, I've gone indie and have published numerous titles for my fledgling publishing house, Braun Haus Media, LLC. I'm also currently working with several other writers who are now published by Braun Haus.

Over the years, I've written several articles on fiction, some of which have been picked up for publication in books on craft, including *Now Write! Mysteries*, and websites like *Creative COW*. My article on creating characters is included as a teaching tool with a screenwriting software package called *Movie Outline*.

One of my craft articles was even plagiarized for a book on screenwriting...

But I won't poke at that particular wound.

And if awards mean anything to you, I won a very prestigious one called *The Nicholl Screenwriting Fellowship*, which is sponsored by the *Academy of Motion Picture Arts & Sciences* (the people who bring you The Oscars), and my thriller, *The Innocent Ones (aka Down Among the Dead Men)*, was nominated for best novel by the *International Thriller Writers*.

Bottom line, over the years I've learned a lot about what works and what doesn't, and formulated my own ideas about how we writers should practice our craft.

What you're about to read are those ideas boiled down to their essence.

But here's the thing I want you to remember as you read on:

These are techniques that work for me.
Your mileage may vary.

Every writer has to find his or her own way.

So I hope you'll take what works for you and discard whatever doesn't.

But, hey, some of you are surely asking yourselves, "Despite all this guy's experience, can he really write, or did he just get lucky?"

I can't answer that question for you.

I happen to think I can write and I'm pretty confident about my proficiency of craft. Confidence is a big, big part of being successful in this business.

But you may not necessarily agree. So, if you have any doubts, check out my novella, *Side Steal*, which I've included at the back of this book. If you think I've got what it takes to teach you a few things about craft, then come back here and dig in.

If not, return the book for a refund and no hard feelings.

Really.

No, really.

WHAT'S THAT TITLE
ALL ABOUT?

What does the title *Casting the Bones* have to do with writing?

Bone divination has been around for centuries and is practiced by many different cultures. Throwing or casting bones is used by psychics who then "read" those bones just as other psychics read palms or tarot cards or tea leaves.

Many years ago, author Harlan Ellison opined that some people outside the profession seem to think writing is magical and that authors cast bones in the dark of night to come up with their stories. The truth, he said, is that writing is simply work.

He certainly wasn't wrong about the work part. Hard work is, without a doubt, the most important ingredient in writing fiction.

But to my mind there's also a little magic there—if only by virtue of the fact that we sometimes need to tap into hidden parts of our brain to find what we need to write a great story. When we go into a kind of trancelike state, and the characters seem to take over and the words are coming out one after another and it almost feels as if we have no control over them.

But don't be fooled. Nine times out of ten, this magic only comes when you know what you're doing. When you understand structure and character and plot and dialogue, and understand it so well that writing becomes as natural to you as walking and talking.

"But wait," you say. "Walking and talking didn't come easily. I had to learn them. I had to practice."

Yes.

We all did.

And every writer you see on the fiction bestseller list had to practice—probably for years—before they wrote the kinds of books that landed them there.

Writing *can* be magic, but that magic only appears when you know what you're doing.

WHAT THIS BOOK IS AND ISN'T

What you are about to read is a series of essays I've written over the years in my attempt to understand the craft of fiction.

This *is not* a book that covers every topic imaginable on the craft.

This *is not* a book that takes you through the steps involved in self-publishing and marketing.

This *is not* a book full of needless prattle in order to fulfill some publisher's idea of how long a book on writing should be.

It *is* brief and to the point and covers just enough of the core tenets of creating fiction that you'll hopefully walk away with a lot of things to think about when you craft your own stories.

I say "craft" for a very specific reason. Because I truly believe the craft of fiction can be learned by anyone. How well is up to you.

The word "art" comes in when someone has used his or her acquired skills and created something so special that few of us can deny it rises to that level.

To my mind, however, the word "artist" is used too carelessly.

We can all aspire to *create* art, but few of us ever achieve that lofty goal.

And you know what? That's okay.

If you can achieve a proficiency of craft that makes people take notice and gets them coming back for more, that's a goal worthy of a lifetime of study and practice.

PRELIMINARIES

*Wherein Rob considers a number
of important questions before we get
into the nuts and bolts of craft.*

1

Indie v. Traditional Publishing

Anyone who reads my Facebook posts knows I have very strong feelings about the way the traditional publishing industry treats authors when it comes to the reversion of rights and the distribution of wealth. But the decision to publish on your own or submit your work through an agent to the Big 5 is an individual one.

If you want to know the good and the bad of either world, there are plenty of resources on the web, but remember, opinions vary based on experience, and no one else's experience will be the same as yours.

For the record, my time in traditional publishing was great. I liked the people I worked with and they treated me with a lot of respect.

When I sold my first four books, traditional publishing was considered the only legitimate path toward publication. Then the Kindle was invented and Amazon opened its doors to authors, and indie pioneers like Joe Konrath and Amanda Hocking started making money hand over fist. And suddenly the idea of self-publishing had great appeal to many authors. Especially those who had been unceremoniously dumped by their publisher when their sales didn't meet some corporate number cruncher's expectations.

When my friend Brett Battles left his publishing house and decided to go indie, I thought he was a little crazy. I was in the middle of finishing up a big, bold, traditionally published "blockbuster" for Dutton that was supposed to set the world on fire.

But then something amazing happened.

Over the course of the next year, Brett started selling a ton of books on Amazon. And as I watched this phenomenon, I couldn't quite believe what I was seeing.

When my Dutton book failed to fly—even after rave national reviews—I wondered if maybe the trad pubs didn't know as much about selling books as they thought they did, and indie was the way to go. The book in question (*The Paradise Prophecy*) was one I would not have chosen to write on my own, but the publisher had come to me, and the advance money had been good, and I'm always a sucker for good advances...

But after its failure to make much of a splash, I wanted to write something for myself. Not for an editor or publisher, but for me. Just me. No restrictions, no dictates from on high, no agent interference, nothing. So I sat down and wrote a book I'd been itching to write for some time. A book that nobody in the industry seemed much interested in. But I wrote it anyway, thinking that I might self-publish it, while still holding onto the idea that maybe I could get a traditional deal instead.

When it was done, however, I looked at all the successful indie authors I knew, saw how well they were doing—and more importantly, how much control over their work they enjoyed—and decided that I definitely needed to give it a shot.

So *Trial Junkies* was published as an indie in May of 2012, and by the middle of June, I was selling nearly a thousand books a day.

I haven't looked back since.

In the years that followed, *Trial Junkies*, has gone on to sell more copies than I ever would have imagined, and the book has received a lot of terrific reviews. It was also picked up by Amazon Crossing for translations to German and French.

So, you see, if you ask me about indie vs. traditional, the answer I'll give you is obvious.

But, as I said, *my* experience may not be yours.

My experience may, in fact, be an anomaly.

So I urge you to do your research and figure out what path is best for you and only you.

2

Are You Really Ready to be a Published Author?

When I was seventeen years old, I wanted nothing more than to be a television writer. I would watch my favorite shows and dream of the day that I'd be putting words into the mouths of my favorite actors.

And that day was coming at any moment.

I could feel it.

My father, who was always my biggest supporter, also thought I was ready and started serving as my "agent." He managed to get a script of mine to the producer of a TV show and the producer was kind enough to read the script and give me some advice.

What he told me was this:

"Your script is overwritten."

And by this he meant that I had put in far too much detail. Added so much information into the narrative that it became a burden to read. We don't need to know every movement a character makes. Keep it simple, keep it direct, and keep it clear.

This was, I believe, the advice that changed my life.

First, it was sound advice. He was absolutely right about my work, and as I look back on that script I see how terrible it really was.

But more importantly, it made me realize that I wasn't as ready to be a published (or produced, in this case) writer as I thought I was. I was blind to my own limitations of craft.

A few years later I met a guy who shared my interest in fiction. He asked me to come over to his apartment to read a novel he'd just finished writing. He knew I was an aspiring author, too, so he figured I'd appreciate reading what he called "a masterpiece."

I was a bit skeptical, of course, but anyone who has that much confidence in his work must surely have something good to show me, so I stopped by to pick up the manuscript.

When I got there he said, "No, no, I don't want you to take it with you. Just sit here and read it."

I balked at the idea, but he insisted, telling me, "Come on, you won't regret it. I promise."

I hesitated, but told him I'd read a couple chapters, then sat down in his easy chair, picked up the manuscript and started reading.

I was no writing expert at the time—was still struggling to find my own voice—but as I read the first few pages, even *I* knew that this guy had done just about everything wrong. Awkward sentences. Lack of clarity. Stilted, "on the nose" dialog. Heavy handed exposition. Rambling, nearly incoherent paragraphs...

And overwriting. Lots of overwriting.

Needless to say, I didn't get very far before I put the manuscript aside.

"What's wrong?" he asked.

I debated whether to be honest with him, then decided that I should be—just as that TV producer had been honest with me. I tried to be as diplomatic about it as possible and told him where I thought the work needed improvement. And without getting into many details, let's just say the guy did not react well.

In fact, for a moment there, I feared for my life. Literally.

Like many writers, this guy was so deep into his belief that he had written a masterpiece that he couldn't take my criticism. And it's *my* belief that if you can't take criticism—at least the constructive kind—then you aren't ready to publish.

Do you for a single moment think your *readers* will be kind?

You don't have to agree with their criticism, of course. I don't make every change my editors suggest. Sometimes I think they're wrong.

But I *do* pay attention. I do realize that whatever notes they give me are meant to help me make the work stronger.

And just like that seventeen year old Rob who thought he was ready to be produced, this guy was convinced that his book was ready to be published. But he had a long, long way to go before he reached that point. And if he never learned to open his mind to helpful criticism, I doubt he ever made much progress.

I've met many people who write their first story or book and think they're ready to take the publishing world by storm. That's a great attitude to have, but you also have to be realistic.

Do yourself a huge favor and step back after you've written something. Take a few days, even a few weeks before you read it again.

This will help give you the perspective and objectivity that you need in order to properly assess the work. Is it good enough? Is it good at all?

Even when I complete a new book (and I've written well over a dozen of them), I'm not fully confident that what I've written is ready to be published. I know I'm able to write a scene and make it read smoothly, but does it all hold together?

Without that small sense of doubt, I think I'd be lost as a writer. Once I'm so confident that what I've written is a masterpiece, I will have taken a step into the same world of make-believe that my friend had.

Now, I'm not trying to make you paranoid here. Your writing may well be *very* publishable. You may be the greatest writer since William Faulkner. But before you get too anxious about buying cover art and throwing the book up on Amazon, be sure to ask yourself if you're ready for it.

Writing publishable work is not something that happens overnight.

Yes, I've met people who seem to have a natural talent and get published very quickly, but this is far outside the norm. Most of us have to write for years before we're producing work that can be looked at as "professional." I myself wrote thousands and thousands of words before I ever even *showed* my work to anyone.

So don't be so anxious to publish. Be anxious to *hone your craft*. Expand your understanding of the process. Write stories that will have readers coming back for more.

Be patient. With time it will come.

3

Practicing Your Magic

My father once took me to a show in Hollywood called *IT'S MAGIC*.

There were about twenty magicians on the bill, one after another showing us their biggest and best tricks, sawing women in half, floating balls in the air and, yes, pulling rabbits out of hats.

I loved the show, and after it was over, my father took me to Bert Wheeler's Magic Shop, where I picked up a trick called multiplying billiard balls.

I practiced that trick for months. And, if I do say so myself, I got pretty good at it. I still have a picture of me—at twelve years old—decked out in the homemade tux my mother made, showing off my sleight of hand dexterity with those Bert Wheeler multiplying balls.

Thing is, the mechanics of the trick weren't very tough. I'm not going to spoil it for you by telling you how it was done, but let's say that just about anyone could do the trick with a few minutes practice.

But I have a feeling it wouldn't look much like magic. It would probably look like some guy ham-handedly struggling to multiply those billiard balls, and the gimmick behind the trick would be obvious to all but the dimmest of spectators.

Real magicians, you see, practice day in and out to make their sleight of hand smooth and undetectable, so that it looks like *real* magic. So that people watch and say, "Wow! Do that again!"

And that's what writers try to do as well. We work very hard behind the scenes, manipulating words and phrases and characters and plot lines—while trying our best to make it all look seamless—in hopes that our readers will say, "Wow! Do that again!"

A lot of people think that all they need to know is how the trick is done and they, too, can be a magician. They're unwilling to put in the real practice necessary, and the moment they learn the move, they're ready to perform.

Writing, like magic, takes years of practice, and a willingness to fail again and again until we get it right, until what we do seems not like simple trickery, but *real* magic to those who read our work. Until our words draw them in and transport them to another time and place, a time and place filled with characters who are alive and breathing and the suspension of disbelief is so deep that we, as writers, can get away with almost anything. Can make them believe that a woman can be cut in half, that rabbits can materialize from nowhere, that those billiard balls can multiply between our fingers...

The great writers, like the great magicians, elevate craft to an art. And as we read their work, we can't help but think, "How did he do that?"

But knowing the "how" is only a small part of the trick. It's knowing what to *do* with that "how" that really counts.

Making the readers believe that what we do is magic.

4

How to Write a Bestseller

I'll say this right up front:

That chapter heading is nonsense

I could have used similar words on the cover of this book to attract those who believe there's some secret ingredient to best-selling fiction, but I didn't.

Why?

Because, first, I like to think I have a little integrity. And second, the truth is, *nobody* can tell you how to write a bestseller.

Nobody.

I don't care if they've sold a gazillion books themselves, there is no person on this planet who can tell you how to write something that will rocket to the bestseller lists.

Not even the big New York publishers know how to get their books on the bestseller lists. If they did, every book they published would be there.

I decided to write this chapter because I was searching the Internet one day and stumbled across a writer's website that had an article with a title very similar to the one above. So I took a look at the post and, yes, the author had included some good advice, but none of it really had anything to do with writing a bestseller. He had simply used that word to get your eyes on the page.

So I used the same trick here to make a point.

And I'll bet your adrenalin rose just a little when you saw it, right?

But here's the thing...

EVERYONE WANTS TO WRITE A BESTSELLER BUT MOST AUTHORS NEVER WILL

Because it's completely out of your control

If you sit down to write a "bestseller," you are taking a wrong-headed approach to writing. Writing great fiction has nothing to do with writing bestsellers. Bestsellers are, by and large, flukes. Right place, right time. And not all bestsellers are created equal.

I can name a dozen of my friends who do everything right and *should* be on the bestseller lists, and authors who *are* and don't belong there.

When I wrote *Trial Junkies*, I just wanted to write a great book. I had no idea it would go on to be an Amazon bestseller. Sure, it was something I hoped for, but I certainly wasn't rubbing my hands together in anticipation of mega-sales. I just wrote the book I wanted to read and decided to let fate take care of the rest.

So don't put all your energy into trying to write a bestseller. You should simply write the best book you can possibly write. A book you're so excited about that you don't care if you ever make a dime off of it.

I spent many years writing stuff that I knew would never sell. In fact, I didn't even *try* to sell it, because I knew it wasn't good enough. But I kept at it for several years. I wrote story fragments and screenplays and teleplays and partial novels and while I knew what I was producing was not quite there yet, I also knew, with great certainty, that it *would* be one day.

Sure, I had dreams of being Stephen King or Dean Koontz. We all do. But the reality is that most writers never make it to the lists, yet they still manage to have wonderful careers.

Should you forget about your dreams?

No. Sometimes they're all you have.

But any thoughts of bestsellerdom should be relegated to the back part of the brain. You have a story to write. And that's *all* you should be thinking about.

If you publish it and it manages to reach one of the bestseller lists, that's just gravy.

So there is no *How* to write a bestseller.

And don't ever be fooled by anyone who claims to know the secret. That particular brand of fairy dust just doesn't exist.

5

Stop Aspiring

Let me put this bluntly.

When aspiring authors ask me the key to writing a book (or a screenplay or a short story or a blog article), my usual response is this:

"AIC."

"AIC?" they say.

"Ass in chair."

Because sitting your butt in that chair in front of your computer, typing one word after another, is the *only* way you're ever going to get a book written.

You can waste a lot of time not writing. Believe me, even pros like me find excuses not to do it. But if you want to stop *thinking* about being a writer and actually *become* one, there's only one way to get there:

Stop aspiring and start perspiring

All right, enough with the lectures.

Let's get to the goods.

THE NUTS AND THE BOLTS
(and maybe a few nails
and some concrete)

*Wherein Rob talks about the techniques
that will make your fiction stand out.*

6

Creating Characters That Jump Off the Page

What I'm about to say is almost blasphemous, but bear with me.

Imagine, if you will, a movie version of *To Kill a Mockingbird* with Will Farrell playing Atticus Finch and a pint-sized Amy Schumer as Scout.

While much of the overall plot could remain intact, the entire flavor of the movie would be radically different than the book and movie we know and love. Scenes would change, dialog would be altered... and despite the plot similarities, chances are pretty good this version would wind up in a completely different category on Netflix.

Which shouldn't surprise anyone.

Because when we watch a movie or read a book it isn't really plot that we invest ourselves in. It's character. The characters set the tone, and our acceptance or rejection of those characters is essential to our acceptance or rejection of the story itself.

Great characters make us laugh and cry or even frustrate and infuriate us. Great characters make us squirm in suspense and excitement. Great characters take us on an emotional rollercoaster ride and are absolutely essential to our suspension of disbelief.

WELL, SURE, BUT...

Whenever I spout off about the all-important need for great characters, someone invariably disagrees. True writing success, they say, lies not only in great characters, but in your ability to come up with a great plot and structure, compelling dialogue and

27

so forth.

And they aren't wrong. In fact, I couldn't agree more.

But the simple truth is this—and I'm not the first to say it:

Your characters define all those things. *They* are your story. Even if you succeed in giving us a wonderful plot and structure, you've got nothing unless your characters jump off the page. In writing fiction of any kind, characters are everything. Everything.

It is impossible to imagine *Gone With the Wind* without the feisty, self-centered yet courageous Scarlett O'Hara. Or *Citizen Kane* without the domineering presence of Charles Foster Kane.

But not only are these lead characters all-important, all the characters who surround them seem to be full-bodied and alive. The authors have somehow managed to pump life into every single character that occupies the page.

Now the question is this: how do you and I do the same thing?

CREATING COMPELLING CHARACTERS

Truth is, I can't tell you how to do this, but I can tell you how *I* do it—and I'm often complimented on my great characters. But my method, like any other method taught out there, is not surefire for everyone who tries it. In fact, many people will reject it out of hand as being far too simplistic. And they may be right. Yet it works for me. And, who knows, it might just work for you.

There are writing gurus who will tell you that the only way to create a great character is to sit down with a legal pad or a bunch of note cards or a character chart and start filling in the blanks.

How old is the character? What's her occupation? What are his likes and dislikes? What school did she graduate from? Where's his hometown? Who were her best friends in grammar school? What kind of parents does he have? Does she have any siblings? The list goes on and on and on.

All of these questions are designed to help you get under the skin of your character. To help you understand him or her to the fullest extent possible so that when you write your scenes, your character will be alive in your own mind. And if he's alive in your own mind, then surely he'll be alive in the minds of your audience.

Well, yes. Of course.

But, I'm sorry, call me lazy, call me stupid—I just can't bring myself to sit down long enough to answer all these questions.

Oh, I've tried. But halfway through I find myself wondering, what's the point to all this? I may say my main character attended Dartmouth—but how exactly does that bit of information help me unless it's directly related to the story at hand?

I have yet to figure it out.

Instead, I approach the task in this way:

CHARACTERS ARE
ATTITUDE

Let's go back to Scarlett O'Hara for a moment. How did I describe her? Feisty, self-centered yet courageous? You could throw in flirtatious and childish as well. These are all attitudes that our audience can immediately latch onto and understand. We don't need to know that she comes from a pampered Southern background and a rebellious Irish father to understand—and perhaps identify with—that attitude. Her attitude alone is enough to draw us in.

Why? Because attitude is action—the character in a state of being. Giving your character an attitude—preferably one that conflicts with the other characters in your story—is a great way to help you and your audience understand who that character is.

CHARACTERS ARE
EMOTION

Adding emotion to your character can help your audience identify with him or her. Looking at Scarlett O'Hara again, when *Gone With the Wind* opens we see the flirtatious and selfish side of Scarlett's personality. But as the opening scenes continue, we discover that despite all the attention she's getting from the men in her world, she's actually in love with another and has been rejected by him. Scarlett is wounded by that rejection yet hides the hurt from all but the object of her affection.

This is an emotion/reaction we can all identify with. If we haven't experienced it ourselves, we have seen it in others we know and love. The emotion is what gives depth to... the attitude.

CHARACTERS
MUST HAVE A GOAL

Every character must have a goal.

Not just the main character. This is a given. Without a goal, your main character will wander aimlessly and your audience will disappear.

But every character that inhabits your story should have a goal. And that character's goal is often what defines both attitude and emotion.

Let's take a relatively minor character for example.

A grocery store clerk.

The hero is buying a carton of milk. For a beat of conflict in an otherwise innocuous scene, we might decide that the grocery store clerk is tired and simply wants to go home. She's been on her feet all day long, the new shoes are killing her and all she wants to do is punch that time clock (and maybe anyone who gets in her way) and get the hell out of there.

This goal can help you define the character's attitude. Is she weary? Is she grouchy? And how does this affect (read: conflict with) the hero?

Giving such a minor character a goal and an attitude/emotion may seem silly, but the result is a much richer story with much richer characters.

CHARACTERS ARE
ACTION / DIALOGUE

Defining an attitude/emotion and a goal are all wonderful, helpful things. But none of them mean squat if we don't see these things in action.

Sure, we can have Joe Blow say our hero is a selfish, manipulating bastard, but that means nothing unless we see this for ourselves. The way your character acts and speaks is what finally defines her/him.

When I describe Scarlett O'Hara as flirtatious and self-centered, these attributes are defined by what Scarlett says and does. She flirts with just about every man who enters her world, she manipulates them into paying attention to her despite the unhappiness this brings to the other women around her. By seeing her in action and hearing her words, we quickly understand the attitude and emotion she brings to the story.

The cliché, *Show Don't Tell*, couldn't be more true here. We must always show our characters acting and reacting—not simply talking about their motivations and desires.

ME + IMAGINATION

Defining a character's goal/attitude/emotion/action are all important, but how exactly do we go about doing that without resorting to those cards and charts and character sketches the writing teachers tell us we so desperately need?

Again, this works for me. It may not work for you. And it's deceptively simple:

Every character I write is me.

From the hero and heroine down to that grocery store clerk, every single character I write is... me.

"Yes," you say, "but isn't that a bit limiting?"

Doesn't that make for a rather monotonous set of characters?

Maybe. But I have yet to hear any complaints. If my lead character is a divorced father of three who finds himself unwittingly involved in a conspiracy to overthrow the government, the first thing I ask myself when approaching a scene (even though I'm happily married and wouldn't know a conspiracy if it jumped up and bit me) is this: how would I react in this situation?

Then I add the color (read: attitude/emotion). How would I react, if... I was a self-centered bastard... a no-nonsense cop... an officious political hack. And I apply this technique to every character I write.

In short, I'm a method actor playing all of the parts.

By using myself and a healthy dose of imagination, I can approach characterization from the inside out. And once I'm able to get into the skin of my characters, it's much, much easier to create someone whom I, and hopefully the audience, can identify with.

FINALLY...

If you still feel you have to drag out the cards and charts, then so be it. If knowing every single little detail about your character is important to you, then by all means write them all down, cover your entire wall with important tidbits of information. I would never belittle anyone for doing what feels right for them.

But while you're at it, take into consideration the things I've talked about here. Remember attitude, emotion, goal and action.

Because these are the things that will make your characters leap off the pages and keep your readers turning them.

7

Building Your Story

Imagine a guy who builds a house on the side of a hill in the Pacific Northwest. Beautiful view. At night, he stands on his deck and looks out at the valley spilling out below him, moonlight reflected on the surface of the ocean beyond.

The house itself is a marvel of wood and glass and filled with just about any convenience you can think of, fully automated by computer.

But a few months after he moves in, the guy's walking barefoot across his carpet when he notices an odd bump in the floor. He explores it with his toes, then crouches down and runs his hands along the bump. Alarmed, he pulls the carpet back and his stomach clutches up when he discovers a crack in the foundation that runs the entire width of the house—a crack that literally splits the place in half.

Frantic calls get him nowhere. He's told very matter-of-factly that the only way to fix it is to tear down the house and start from scratch with a new foundation. It turns out the original foundation was improperly laid and couldn't withstand the weight of the house.

Now, a week later, the storm of the decade washes half of his house into the valley. Pieces of the guy's dream are scattered from his perch on the mountainside all the way to the Pacific Ocean.

Despondent, the guy moves in with a friend who tells him, "Can't build a house without a solid foundation."

And he's right. You can't. And you shouldn't.

The same applies to fiction.

Writing a story is like building a house. Without a solid foundation, it's bound to fall apart.

And by foundation, I mean the underlying structure.

That underlying structure is one of the most important parts of any story.

Remember that.

Burn it into your brain.

WHAT STRUCTURE IS

When people ask writers what structure is, the most common response you hear is this: a beginning, middle and end.

Well, duh. We've all seen enough movies and read enough books to know that you've gotta start somewhere, end somewhere else, and that a bunch of stuff has to happen in between. Otherwise what's the point?

The trick is knowing *where* to start, *where* to end, and *what* to put in between.

Several years ago I read an article in Writer's Digest by a writer named Gary Provost. Mr. Provost wisely compared a story to a basketball game, in which the players have an overall goal—to win the game.

To reach that goal, they must face the challenge of several smaller goals, traveling from one end of the court to another in order to score points and, of course, to prevent the opposing team from scoring.

All during the game, the two teams have conflicting goals and will do anything they can to stop the other from succeeding.

Mr. Provost was, I believe, trying to describe the nature of conflict in storytelling, and he did it in a way that not only tells us about conflict, but about structure as well. The two are so closely intertwined that it would be difficult not to discuss them both in the same breath.

Structure is a series of goals—or navigating points—that lead to an overall goal. You can't have your players wandering around for no reason. They have to have a purpose in life. They have to know what their objectives are and must be willing to fight to reach those objectives.

A MAN WITH A PURPOSE

Let's look for a moment at the movie *The Fugitive.*

It's been around for over twenty years, is based on a once popular television show, so there's a good chance you either saw it when it was released in theaters, watched the DVD, or you've seen it when it popped up on cable TV. While not a perfect action-thriller, it comes pretty close, especially in terms of structure.

It opens with a woman being killed. Her husband, a prominent doctor, is arrested and convicted for her murder, but he's an innocent man. The real killer is a one-armed man he fought with at the crime scene.

On the way to prison, there's a terrible bus crash and the doctor escapes just as a train slams into the bus. Seizing this opportunity, he begins his quest to clear his name. And the only way to do this is to find the one-armed man.

This setup is the "beginning" of the story. Act One. It defines the main character, his situation, and his overall goal, which is to find the one-armed man who killed his wife. Not only is this the *character's* overall goal, it was the *writer's* as well. And it was the writer's job to figure a way to get his hero to this goal in a dramatically compelling way.

Not an easy task.

To accomplish that, the writer structured a series of sub-goals that would eventually lead his hero to the end of the game. Conflict helped him do that.

Let's break it down:

In Act One of *The Fugitive*, what is the first sub-goal? What dramatically compelling event did the writer have to reach to keep this story moving?

I'll give you a hint:

To get Dr. Kimble arrested.

Kimble's wife is killed, he fights with the one-armed man, the one-armed man escapes and Kimble is left behind with no alibi and blood on his clothes. The next thing he knows he's arrested for murder.

In the process of setting up the character's main objective, the writer used this smaller goal as a kind of navigating point. And by breaking the act down to a *series* of subgoals/navigating points, the writer was able to execute his story in more manageable chunks.

The second sub-goal in Act One of *The Fugitive* is what?

To get Kimble convicted of the murder.

And this is followed by a third, and slightly bigger goal:

To free Kimble from custody.

This final sub-goal—precipitated by the bus and train crash—ends Act One and allows Kimble to begin his quest toward his overall objective.

GOALS, GOALS AND MORE GOALS

The part of the story that usually makes or breaks the writer is the "middle" part, or Act Two.

This act is commonly known as the confrontation act, and carries the bulk of the story. Again, like Mr. Provost's basketball game, Act Two is filled with many sub-goals and, hopefully, a formidable force to keep the hero from reaching those goals.

In *The Fugitive*, Kimble has escaped at the end of Act One, but Act Two brings him a whole new series of problems.

His immediate objective is to get to safety and to take care of a gash in his side caused by the bus wreck. He runs through the woods in his prison garb, exchanges it for a truck driver's overalls, then sneaks into the nearest hospital and tends to the wound.

These scenes are filled with conflict because Kimble is being pursued at the time by a new character the writer has introduced: Kimble's nemesis, U.S. Marshall Sam Gerard, a hard-assed fugitive hunter.

Gerard's overall goal is to bring his man in. He's the opposing team, trying to score points and win the game.

So in Act Two, the first sub-goal is this:

Getting Kimble to the hospital.

This sub-goal arises from the conflict preceding it—the bus crash, the wound in his side, and police pursuit—as Kimble reacts to and battles against them.

This, in turn, leads to yet another sub-goal or navigating point:

The first confrontation between Kimble and Gerard.

After patching himself up at the hospital, Kimble steals an ambulance, gets cornered by Gerard in a viaduct and jumps to certain death in order to escape. Again, by using this first confrontation as a navigating point and writing toward it, the writer was better able to manage his story.

Since we're limited by space here, rather than continue through the story scene by scene, let's look at some of the sub-goal/navigating points that helped the writer make it through Act Two:

Kimble survives the jump and heads back to Chicago.

He contacts a colleague, who helps him with money.

He goes to the prosthetic ward of a Chicago hospital and gets a list of one-armed men.

He calls several of the men, narrows down the list, and discovers one is in prison.

He goes to the prison, discovers it's the wrong guy, but is confronted by Gerard and must escape.

He breaks into the apartment of the last man on his list and finds photos and evidence that raise questions about a drug Kimble's own hospital had been testing, a drug Kimble knew was defective.

He goes to his hospital to investigate and discovers his colleague was behind his wife's murder—with Kimble the intended target.

Each of these is a sub-goal/navigating point that helps the writer build his story. Moving parallel to this are a series of goals involving the Gerard character. By moving from one to the next, the writer is able to build a series of sequences, each affected by one preceding it.

By going beyond the simple "beginning, middle and end" and structuring your own story this way, your foundation becomes as solid as a rock, and the process is much easier to handle.

Like those before it, Act Three, the resolution, will have its own navigating points, the biggest of all being the hero's success or failure to achieve his overall goal.

Have your eyes glazed over yet?

Hey, nobody said writing is easy.

AND IT DOESN'T STOP THERE

Structure doesn't end with these navigating points. When we break our story down further, each scene should have a goal and a structure of its own.

That's right.

In a well-written story, each scene has its own setup, confrontation and resolution. These elements won't be as fully formed as they are in the overall story, but they're there. I urge you to take a very close look at any well-written novel (or movie) and see for yourself.

THE LONG AND WINDING ROAD

Anybody confused?

I hope not.

For those of you who are, simply think of what it's like to drive across country. It would be impossible to take the trip in one long haul, never stopping to rest and refuel.

Before we get started, most of us fire up our GPS, punch in our destination and look for navigation points along the way to break up the monotony of a long journey.

So, go on, get out of here. Mark your route and start driving. And whatever you do, don't get lost.

8

Against the Wind

Imagine this scene from a story:

It's 1983. A woman sits behind a typewriter, finishing up a page. When she's done, she types THE END, pulls the page out and adds it to a large stack next to her on the desk.

She smiles, then goes to a liquor cabinet, pulls out a bottle, and pours a drink to toast a job well done.

All is good in her world.

Now imagine this one instead:

It's 1983. A woman sits behind a typewriter, crying her eyes out as she finishes up a page and types THE END. She pulls the page out, adds it to the stack on her desk, but she's crying so hard that she has to blow her nose. She reaches for a tissue, but the box is empty. So she gets up, still sobbing, and goes to the bathroom, looking for some toilet paper. The roll is empty.

Moving about the house, she steps into the kitchen and grabs a post-it note off the refrigerator—one that says BUY TOILET PAPER —and uses it to blow her nose.

Then, moving back into her living room, she opens a cabinet, pulls out a tiny bottle of "airplane" liquor, intending to use it for a toast to celebrate finishing her book, but when she tries to get the cap off, it won't budge. It takes all of her strength to get the cap loose and she finally makes her toast.

And despite this celebration, it's quite obvious that this woman is a complete and utter mess.

Okay.

Now, tell me, which of these scenes would you rather watch?

Me, I'll go with the second one. In fact I have, in a wonderful movie from the eighties called *Romancing the Stone*. And I think most people would be much less inclined to fall asleep during version two than they would if subjected to version one.

Version one just sits there. *Lays* there, in fact.

Why?

Because it has no conflict.

Conflict is the cornerstone of good storytelling. Conflict is what grabs our interest, makes us want to continue reading. And this isn't just limited to movies and novels.

How many of us would watch the news if all we saw were happy, feel-good stories? People *thrive* on conflict, and anyone who thinks a story doesn't need it, is completely out of touch with what good, solid storytelling is all about.

Your basic plot line—no matter what kind of book you're writing—always centers around characters in conflict. There's usually both an internal conflict *and* an external one. And the external conflict should challenge or contribute to the character's internal conflict (and probably vice versa).

If you give me a story about two people sailing through life without a care in the world, then I might as well watch paint dry. I need something in that story to grab me by the heart or the throat. To give rise to my emotions. To make me laugh and cry and root for the hero. And if all the hero is doing is contemplating his or her navel, then, please, get me the hell out of there.

Your characters must have a goal—no matter how trivial it might seem—and they must have strong opposition to that goal.

Even the simple act of searching for a way to blow her nose makes the second scenario above the more compelling one.

I can't say this enough. Conflict is one of the most essential elements of telling a good story. And sharing that moment when a character overcomes conflict is what lifts us. What thrills us. What sends us soaring.

As Hamilton Mabie once said, "A kite rises against, not with, the wind."

9

What if?

One of the best ways to construct a plot is to use a very simple technique that almost makes the process seem effortless.

All you have to do is ask yourself a series of "What-Ifs."

What if a Neo-Nazi terrorist organization got hold of a nuclear bomb?

What if they planted that bomb in an American football stadium?

What if a fledgling CIA analyst uncovered the plan and couldn't convince his superiors that he was right?

What if the bomb actually went off, destroying half an American city?

What if the terrorists planted evidence making it look like the Russians were at fault?

As you can see, this series of What Ifs practically lays out the structure of the movie version of Tom Clancy's *The Sum of All Fears*. And as we plot out What-Ifs like these and turn them into scene and sequence, each and every one of them forms a question in the reader's mind.

Let's look at some of them again:

What if a Neo-Nazi terrorist organization got hold of a nuclear bomb?

(Reader: Oh, no, what are they going to do with it?)

What if they planted the bomb in an American football stadium?

(Reader: Oh my God, will someone stop it before it explodes?)

What if a fledgling CIA analyst uncovered the plan and couldn't convince his superiors that he was right?
(Reader: Oh crap, how will he stop them?)

Each *What-If* you present, each question you put into the mind of your reader, helps compel her forward through the story. She turns the page for one simple reason: she wants to find out what will happen next.

The longer you take to reveal the answers to these questions, the stronger the hold you'll have on your audience. It's important not to give away too much too soon, or your audience will have nothing to look forward to.

You must always remember to take the revelations slow. Don't be too anxious to give it away. And as you answer each of these story points, make sure you replace them with questions that are even more compelling.

Every story—no matter what genre—should be an unfolding mystery.

10

Wonderful World of Subplots

While you can certainly get away with a short story having only one plot, novels will almost always have a number of plots going at once. One of those plots is dominant, of course, but what about those smaller, all important sub plots?

In *The Godfather*, we watch as a violent power play is made against Don Corleone by a rival Mafia family. His young, clean-cut son, Michael Corleone, volunteers to take revenge, and the movie follows Michael's descent into the dark world of the Mafia and his eventual emergence as the new Godfather.

There are a number of subplots in the movie, but the one that most strikes a chord is Michael's relationship with two women. The first is Kay, who is not Italian, not part of the "family" and is Michael's lifeline to the outside world. His connection to "reality."

But as he's drawn deeper into the violence, Michael's ties to her become more and more tenuous, until he finds himself completely cut off from her—and the outside world—as he hides out in Sicily.

In Sicily, Michael meets a young local woman who steals his heart. She's his soul mate, his true love, whom he marries. Then, in another act of revenge, a car carrying his new bride is blown to bits, plunging Michael into an emotional darkness he's never known.

He goes back to the U.S. a considerably different man, but rekindles his relationship with Kay and eventually marries her—a marriage that is obviously doomed.

This particular subplot would probably have a tough time standing on its own. Its reliance on the main storyline is obvious enough, but what really makes it great is that it parallels and impacts Michael's descent. Kay represents Michael's relationship to the "civilian" world, while his marriage to the Sicilian woman illustrates his rediscovery of his roots.

The tragic twist in this subplot is one of the major causes of Michael's emotional retreat and his rise to power. He becomes a man so cold and ruthless that he's able (in *Part II*) to put a hit out on his own brother...

And that's what all great movie and novel subplots do. They rise organically from the main storyline, attaching themselves to your hero and impacting his ability to reach his goal. Great subplots are so closely woven into the fabric of the story that we often have a hard time discerning them.

Even so-called "lesser" movies than *The Godfather* recognize the need for a solid subplot.

A favorite of mine is a dark thriller called *Resurrection*, which was written by Brad Mirman, the writer of several good thrillers. To some, *Resurrection* plays like a poor man's rip-off of *Seven*, but I much prefer Mirman's take on the hunt for a serial killer because of its inventiveness.

Resurrection is essentially about a couple of cops hunting for a serial killer who is taking the body parts of his victims and building them into a representation of Christ. Each of the victims is named after an apostle and the killer's timeline runs him straight toward Easter, the day of resurrection.

The subplot is a minor one, but it certainly deepens the lead character. He's a cop who, after the tragic death of his son, has discarded his faith in God and is quickly losing his emotional connection to his wife.

During the course of the movie, his wife attempts to repair their marriage and his faith by inviting the local priest over for a pep talk, but our hero soundly rejects the man and any notion of accepting help from him.

Then, while looking for a clue to the killer's plan that seems deeply rooted in Biblical lore, our hero must finally seek the help of the priest. But as he enters the church, he hesitates, as if the mere act of stepping foot in the place is a betrayal of his son's memory.

Again, this subplot is powerful because it is so securely attached to the main storyline that it can't exist on its own. The two plots feed off of each other and both are stronger because of it.

A lot of books today treat subplots as an afterthought. Stories are often built based on a "hot" idea, the characters created to fill out a plot that's stretched so thin that the slightest jolt could snap it apart.

Subplots are haphazardly tacked on in a weak attempt to keep the whole mess together, and their paint-by-numbers obviousness is one of the greatest contributors to the collective snore rising from the readers.

Many storytellers today have it backwards. Yes, start with a great idea, but rather than try to force characters and subplot into that story, try creating the characters first, then let the story and subplot grow from them.

Characters are story. And any great plot or subplot is driven by the characters' wants and desires.

Remember this as you sit down to write and, with time and patience, you too can give us writing the caliber of *The Godfather* and *Resurrection.*

Not a bad place to be.

11

Seducing Your Readers

Let's talk about sex. Those of you who are uncomfortable with the subject, feel free to bail out now. I'm likely to get pretty raunchy.

Still with me? I thought so.

When we make love, most of us have a particular goal in mind: that moment when our entire body seems to stem from one central point, when every nerve-ending tingles wildly as fireworks assault our brain.

That moment, of course, is orgasm, and anyone who has experienced one (or two or three)—especially with a willing and enthusiastic partner (or two or three)—knows that it can be an exquisitely pleasurable sensation.

But are all orgasms created equal?

Of course not. The quality of our orgasms is directly related to the quality of the fun and games that precede them, not to mention our emotional bond with our partner, and our willingness (or unwillingness) to surrender ourselves fully to the moment.

So *what*, you're probably wondering, does any of this have to do with writing?

YOUR WILLING PARTNER

Writing is an extremely intimate act. In his book, *On Writing*, Stephen King describes it as a form of telepathy. You put your thoughts on paper, and days, months, or even years later, someone reads your mind.

Think about it. With a simple arrangement of words, you have the potential to pull our audience into your mind where they can be stroked and fondled and toyed with—sometimes gently, sometimes rough.

The result is often a partnership so strong and emotionally satisfying that neither of us ever wants to let go.

Who of us here can forget those times when we've read a book we didn't want to end? And when the end did come, we felt drained, elated, and thoroughly satisfied, much like we do after a night of unbridled passion.

Getting to that place wasn't an accident. The writer of the book —at least in most cases—didn't merely fumble his way toward climax. If he (or she) did his job, every step was carefully choreographed to lead us around the third act corner toward the final pay-off.

And the quality of that pay-off is related to one important thing:

THE GENTLE ART OF LOVEMAKING

We're often reminded in how-to books that the typical story is broken into three acts: Set-up, Confrontation, and Resolution. I've already talked about this in the chapter on building your story.

But it sounds pretty cold and uncaring, doesn't it? Not to mention dull.

But what if we were to beat the lovemaking analogy into the ground and refer to the three acts in this way:

Seduction, Foreplay, and Climax.

That certainly puts a whole new slant on things, doesn't it? And if we're to have a successful story with a successful and satisfying ending—one that keeps our partners wanting more—we must pay careful attention to these three words.

Seduction.

The beginning of a story, any story, cannot and should not be referred to as anything other than a seduction. It is our job to make our audience want us.

How do we accomplish that?

First we start with character. We must create characters that our audience won't mind, figuratively speaking, getting into bed with. Particularly the lead.

Is he or she someone we find attractive?

Does he have a problem or flaws we can relate to?

Are his life circumstances universal yet unique enough to pique our interest?

The next element is mystery. As I said previously, every story should be a mystery.

Remember the girl in college the guys all wanted but knew so little about? A big part of her allure was the hint of mystery she carried.

No matter what genre you're writing in, you should never, never, never put all of your cards on the table at the beginning of the game. Instead you must reveal them one at a time, each new card offering a clue to the mystery of our characters and their stories.

The third and most important element of seduction is giving your characters a goal. And, again, not just your lead. Every single character you write should have a goal of some kind. Put two characters with opposing goals in a room and you have drama.

But the goal of your hero must be compelling enough to intrigue us and hold our interest.

Foreplay.

Once we get our reader into bed, however, we certainly can't let them down. As you would with a lover, you explore and tease and make new discoveries—which can often lead your partner to discover something about his or herself that, until that moment, remained dormant.

The foreplay in the second act is a continuation of the seduction but on a deeper, more intimate level. This is when we really begin to understand and root for the characters, and when their stake in the outcome becomes more and more important. Surprises are sprung, secrets are revealed, and our emotions and feelings build with each new scene, gradually working us toward the moment we're all waiting for:

The Climax.

And this is why we're here today, class, to talk about that most crucial of Act Three moments: the time when all of the work you've done for the last three hundred or so pages comes together like the pieces of a puzzle, where plot and subplot intertwine to create the only ending that makes sense within the context of the story you've told—a thrilling and, hopefully, explosive orgasm of emotion.

The final kiss; the final death; the final revelation that sends your audience soaring.

But you can't get there without laying the proper groundwork.

Author Mickey Spillane once said that the first page of a novel sells that novel and the last page sells the next one. This is certainly true, but what he doesn't say is that what comes between is what sells that last page. Without masterful seduction and foreplay it is virtually impossible to reach a satisfying climax.

Act Three is a culmination of all that came before it, and if the preceding two acts are anything short of spectacular, you'll be lucky if your readers even stick around for number three.

It's all up to you.

Every time you sit down to write, you must remember that the reader is your partner, your lover, and in order to make him or her happy you must seduce, thrill, and most importantly, satisfy.

12

Hooking Your Readers

There have long been hooks in fiction.

Back in the old days, serialized fiction in newspapers and magazines had them. The end of each installment had you hooked—wanting to read the next installment *right now*.

When movies came along the old twelve-reeler serials always ended with the hero or heroine in dire straits—sometimes literally dangling from the edge of a cliff—which had the kiddies anxious for the next installment. These hooks became what's known as a cliffhanger.

You see the same thing on television today. You have the commercial cliffhangers, the weekly cliffhangers and the season cliffhangers.

For those who were around and cognizant during the original version of *Dallas*, the most famous cliffhanger of all was "who shot JR?"

The season ended with oil baron JR Ewing being shot by an unseen assailant, and everyone went nuts over the summer hiatus, rocketing *Dallas* into the stratosphere of popular television shows.

A more recent show is *Homeland.*

Wow.

Not only is it well acted and directed, it's smartly written and shot—an all around great show that I watch for inspiration simply because I think the writing is so smart. It's the perfect show to illustrate all the best tricks of writing that television/movie writers use. And each episode ends with such a compelling hook that you can't wait to see the next one.

Obviously, books are the perfect place to do this. If you read one of my thrillers, you'll find that I end almost every chapter with some kind of hook. Something that kicks things up a bit and makes the reader think, "Oh, damn. Just one more chapter and I'll go to bed."

And, of course, that's what I want them to think. The best emails I ever get are the ones in which the reader tells me she's mad at me because I made her stay up all night.

I'm a manipulative bastard.

But such hooks aren't limited to thrillers. Love stories are full of them. Mysteries. Literary fiction. Sometimes they can be in your face and sometimes they can be subtle. The key is to give the reader enough of a kick to keep them wanting to read.

So, where can we find examples?

Watch a lot of serialized television. You will learn so much from them, even the bad ones, which should teach you what *not* to do.

I also invite you to take a look at one of my books. (I would, wouldn't I?) The chapter endings in, say, *Kiss Her Goodbye,* are not exactly in your face, but they're definitely designed to keep you reading.

But you don't have to read just my books. Pick up other writers' books and pay close attention to their chapter endings. If you find yourself losing interest, then they haven't done their job. But if you find that you're unable to keep from turning to the next chapter, chances are good they've grabbed you with a cliffhanger of some kind.

And that's how page turners are made.

13

More Thoughts on the Hook

The first few pages of a book are absolutely crucial to the success of that work.

That's a bold statement, sure, but true. If you do not hook your reader in your first few pages, it is unlikely that they'll continue reading.

So how, exactly, *do* you hook them? I have a few ideas:

YOUR VOICE

Every writer has a unique voice. A particular way of saying things that makes us know right away who's writing.

Stephen King is a great example.

Years ago, when he wrote *Thinner* under the pen name Richard Bachman, I remember picking up the book in the bookstore and thinking, jeez, this guy writes just like Stephen King.

And it was good, of course. I was hooked from page one. If you work to develop a voice that is smooth, professional and, most importantly, entertaining, you'll have gone a long way toward making those first ten pages sing.

MAKE IT A MYSTERY

As I've said a number of times now, I don't care what kind of story you're writing, *every* story is a mystery story. And by mystery, I merely mean that you don't reveal everything up front.

You tease your reader, planting questions in his/her mind, questions that he wants answers to. But then you take your time answering them.

In a typical cop story, this might be "Who killed the waiter and why?"

But it could also be "Who rejected Allison? Why is she afraid to ride the bus? What happened to her that was so traumatic?"

Your job is to plant seeds in those first few pages and use the next three hundred or so to watch them grow.

START WITH ACTION

And by action I don't necessarily mean a chase scene or gun play. I merely mean to begin *in motion*.

You might have a couple waiting to hear from a doctor, or a man driving to a place he's dreading, a woman getting a phone call from an old lover.

Whatever the case, do not start with a stagnant scene—like someone waking in the morning.

Start with the story already in motion. Almost as if the reader has entered the movie theater a minute or so late and has to puzzle out why the hero is doing what he's doing.

If you follow these three suggestions, I think you'll be a long way toward making those first few pages engaging and rewarding to the reader.

But once you've got them hooked, the trick is to keep them hooked until the very last scene.

14

Enter Late, Leave Early

There is an old screenwriting trick that works just as well for novels and short stories. It's a great way to keep your scenes moving, giving your work that page-turning urgency that keeps readers reading.

It's called *Enter Late/Leave Early*.

When writing a scene, rather than start at the "beginning," try entering the scene late—coming in after events are already in motion. Then make sure you get out of there before said events have concluded.

For example:

John and Mary decide to go for a jog. Instead of cutting to the two of them throwing on their jogging shorts, pulling on their running shoes, and hitting the road, we cut straight to John and Mary running side by side, in the middle of a conversation.

Then, once the point of the scene has been made, we cut away from them *before* they finish their jog *or* their conversation. And to compel the reader forward, it often helps to use a line of dialogue or prose that's a springboard into the next scene.

Brevity is extremely important in screenplays and short stories, but it's important in novels as well. The last thing you want to do is bore your reader. While novels give you more room to explore character motivation, background and feelings, in the days of modern novel writing, it's important to keep things moving.

Any good story should have rhythm, aided by the ebb and flow of your scenes. And *Enter Late/Leave Early* is one way to maintain that rhythm.

Get in, make your point, then get the heck out.

15

On the Nose

I was recently sitting with a friend who asked me what I thought of a big bestselling author.

My response was, "People seem to love him."

"That isn't what I asked," my friend said. "What do *you* think of him?"

I hesitated, because while there was a time I would openly criticize writers, those days are long gone. Partly because I'm not immune to criticism myself and partly because I'm in a business that requires a certain etiquette, and I'm learning to be polite.

So, I simply said, "For me—and this is my opinion only—his writing is too on the nose."

Then came the usual question. "What the heck does that mean?"

"It's a Hollywood term," I said, "for when everything is right up front, in your face. There's no nuance or subtlety, no subtext. What you see is what you get, as if you're being tapped on the nose."

The big bestselling author in question, often writes things like this:

The evil killer watched them from a hill overlooking the house.
He was going to kill them all.

Now there's nothing particularly wrong with that, I suppose. But, for me, it's painfully matter of fact. It tells the reader exactly what he needs to know without making him or her work at it.

And, to my mind, the reader should always have to do a little work, because writing is all about *shared imagination.* The author gives the readers just enough information to allow their imaginations to take over and fill in the blanks.

MAKE YOUR STORY A PUZZLE

I always think of a story as a puzzle. Your job as a writer is to supply the pieces of the puzzle and enough juice behind them to get the reader to want to put those pieces together and figure out what picture they form.

So rather than tell them that the guy on the hill is an evil killer, you instead put that guy on the hill, but you don't tell them who he is, why he's there, or what his plans are.

You only give them *one* piece of the puzzle.

Then, somewhere in the next several pages you might mention Joe's missing brother Johnny. Johnny hasn't been seen in three years and nobody knows where he went after he escaped the police while being transported to jail on a murder charge.

Put those pieces together and your reader is pretty much figuring that the guy on the hill is Johnny. Or, if it isn't Johnny, he certainly had something to do with the guy—or maybe even Johnny's disappearance.

Who knows? You'll only find out if you continue to read.

The point, of course, is that by not telling them everything up front, you create something *very* important in your reader:

The desire to learn more.

And once they have that desire, they will not stop until they satisfy it.

If you spell it all out for them right up front, however, what have you created?

A reader who's about to delete the book from the Kindle.

Then again, maybe I'm wrong.

Because on the nose or not, that big bestselling author sells books like crazy.

Is it because people think he's a terrific storyteller or because they just don't want to bother to do any work? Maybe some readers (or even a lot of them) just don't have any interest in figuring anything out and want to be spoon fed the story without

having to think too much.
    The readers I know aren't like that.
    I know *I'm* not like that.
    But this guy *does* have a lot of fans.
    Maybe you should go take a Masterclass on writing by him...

16

Leaving Out the Parts People Skip

Elmore Leonard, one of our best American writers, famously said that he tried to "leave out the parts people skip" when he was writing. Anyone who has read a Leonard novel knows that they are lean, move quickly, and certainly don't require any skimming.

But what exactly does that mean?

People start skimming when they lose interest. When they want you to get on with things. When they're not as engaged by the story as they should be.

So how do you keep them engaged?

What follows are a few ideas. I've talked about some of them in previous chapters (maybe more than once), but feel I should repeat them here for emphasis.

KEEP YOUR PROSE STYLE
SIMPLE, ECONOMIC, AND CLEAR

You can certainly be clever and artistic, but never sacrifice economy and clarity for the sake of "art." Much of that art, in fact, is writing in a way that the sentences and paragraphs and pages flow from one to the next, giving the reader no choice but to hang onto every word.

And clarity is always important. If a reader is confused about what is going on, she may well give up on you.

Don't bog your story down with too much description.

Descriptive passages can be quite beautiful, but your job is to weigh whether or not they're necessary. Poetic writing is often wonderful, but those who can pull it off are rare.

Gregory MacDonald, the author of the *Fletch* books, among others, once said that because we live in a "post-television" world, it is no longer necessary to use the amount of description needed in the past. We all know what the Statue of Liberty looks like because we've seen it on TV. We've seen just about everything on TV, and probably even more on the Internet.

So, I think it's best to limit your descriptions to only what is absolutely necessary to make the story work. Meaning: enough to set the scene, set up a character, or to *clarify* an action.

Let's face it. Saying something as simple as, *The place was a dump. Several used syringes lay on the floor next to a ratty mattress with half its stuffing gone* is often more than enough to get the message across.

If you can, describe a setting through the eyes of whatever character controls the scene (meaning point of view). If you include the description as part of that character's thought process, colored by his or her mood or personality, the description then becomes much more dynamic and also reveals a lot about that character.

One man's dump, after all, may be another man's paradise. And showing how a character reacts to a place is much more interesting than a static description.

TEASE YOUR READERS

I know, I know, I keep hammering this point home, because I think it's an essential one.

One of the biggest mistakes I see aspiring writers make is that they try to reveal too much about character motivation and story too soon. Your job—as crass as it might sound—is to manipulate your reader. To keep her reading. Turning those pages.

Imagine meeting someone for the first time and they tell you everything there is to know about them. Where they were born, where they went to school, how many affairs they've had, how many brothers and sisters, their favorite color, their favorite food —you get the point.

What makes people interesting to us is that all of these things are revealed over a long period of time. We get to know them gradually, rather than all at once. They are a mystery that we have to unravel.

The same holds true with storytelling. You manipulate your readers by constantly creating questions in their minds. Why is she doing that? Where is she going? What happened to her in the past that makes her afraid of confronting him?

If we know it all up front, we'll lose interest fast.

GIVE YOUR CHARACTERS
A SERIES OF GOALS

Most stories will involve a central character who wants something. In a thriller, for instance, that may be something very big. The hero wants to stop the bad guy from, say, blowing up the federal building.

But if that's all the story is about, then I'm yawning already.

If you give the hero a series of goals, smaller points he or she must reach—both internally and externally—before finally reaching that ultimate goal, then your reader will never lose interest.

A great example is the third *Die Hard* movie, *Die Hard with a Vengeance.*

The bad guy has something nefarious up his sleeve. But in order to distract the police from that ultimate goal, he sends them on a series of wild goose chases involving high explosives. And because our heroes are moving from one goal to the next, we're never bored. In fact, we spend much of our time on the edge of our seat.

In the meantime, the main hero suspects that something is up, and as he tries to puzzle it out, we're right there with him. We have only as much information as he has, so we're not about to abandon ship until he (and we) knows the truth.

But more importantly, we also have a dynamic relationship playing out on screen between two characters played by Bruce Willis and Samuel L. Jackson. These two men must work together reluctantly, and because we find them engaging, our stake in the outcome of the story is even higher.

Which brings me to my final point:

CREATE COMPELLING CHARACTERS

If you don't create characters who are interesting in themselves, who have internal struggles we can relate to, who have fears we understand, who have a goal that makes sense to us on a personal level, then it doesn't matter how cleverly you plot your novel. We won't care.

If you need help creating compelling characters, take a look at the chapter on *Creating Characters that Jump Off the Page.*

Hopefully all of the above will help you "leave out the parts people skip." And if you want to find out how the master himself does it, go pick up an Elmore Leonard novel today.

But be warned. He does it so well, it's seamless. So you'll have to pay close attention...

17

Point of View

As a boy experiencing my first thrills reading fiction, I read a lot of pulp novels, like the reissued versions of *The Shadow* that came out in the early seventies in paperback.

I loved those stories, but even at the time, I knew there was nothing particularly special about the writing. It was serviceable prose that did the job it needed to do and I loved the adventures of Kent Allard turned Lamont Cranston turned The Shadow.

But the stories that *really* grabbed me very early on were the comedy crime thrillers of Donald Westlake, particularly his stand alones like *Somebody Owes Me Money* and *The Fugitive Pigeon*.

Both of those books were written in first person and the immediacy of that point of view never failed to grab hold of me. And whenever I came upon a book that wasn't written in first person, I was disappointed.

It didn't keep me from reading, mind you, but I was a tried and true first person reader in those early days and my first attempts at writing were from that point of view.

By the time I wrote my first complete novel—which was many, many years later—I had gotten over my love affair with particular points of view and simply learned that a good book is a good book and point of view is largely dependent on what *kind* of story you're writing.

That first novel was written in third person. Very close third person. But with chapters from different points of view. I have since written novels (under pen names) in first person as well, and loved every minute of it.

I'm not going to get too deeply into this, because the point of view you choose for your story is really a choice only you can make. It should be the point of view that pops into your brain when you begin to form the first sentences of the work.

And if it works, it works. If it doesn't, try again from a different point of view.

My main reason for including this chapter is this:

If you *do* choose to write in third person, there's one mistake that many authors make that drives me—and I think most readers —completely nuts.

So I ask you:

PLEASE, FOR THE SAKE OF
ALL THAT IS HOLY...

DO NOT **JUMP HEADS**

If you're writing a scene from Joe's point of view and he's talking to Gina, *please, please, please*, stay inside Joe's head until that scene is over. Avoid the temptation to tell us what Gina is thinking, because Joe's on stage now and we're "listening" to his thoughts and any sudden jumps into Gina's head will be jarring and, frankly, unprofessional.

Oh, sure, there are professionals who do this. And unless they're so good at it that I hardly notice (although it's hard *not* to), I'll stop reading.

If there is one hard and fast rule in all of this book it's that one.

DO NOT HEAD JUMP IN THE
MIDDLE OF A SCENE.
EVER.
FOR ANY REASON.

I don't care if your favorite author in the world does it. He or she should take a refresher course in fiction and be banned from the practice.

If you're in the middle of a scene and you *really* feel you have to be in Gina's head for awhile, there's one simple way to take care of that desire:

Double space.

That's right. Skip down a couple spaces to indicate to the reader that you're shifting gears a bit and are now entering Gina's head, where you will stay for awhile until you feel the need to double space again—or go to a whole new chapter—so that Joe can once again have his say.

I cannot emphasize this enough.

Seriously.

Don't do it.

I beg you.

18

Crafting Dialogue

One of the toughest nuts to crack in fiction writing is dialogue.

You can have the most wonderful voice in the world, your narrative may sing on the page, but if your dialogue lays there, sucking the life out of everything around it, you're in huge trouble.

Here are a few tips to help you make your dialogue sing.

BREAKING IT UP

When I first started out, writing dialogue did not come naturally. I had a tendency to write long passages of speech, characters talking for literally paragraphs. This, I've discovered, is a common problem with novice writers. So I certainly wasn't alone.

For example, imagine coming across this in a book or movie:

"Look, Joey, I don't care what you say, I'm not going in there. You hear me? I haven't seen Sarah in fifteen years and I'll be damned if I'm going to face her now, after what I did to her. I mean, for Christ's sake, do I look like an idiot? Do I look like somebody who enjoys being humiliated? I guarantee the first thing she'd do is spit in my face. And I wouldn't blame her. Would you? I pretty much ruined her life."

Now, I don't suppose the dialogue above is all that bad. But is this monologue really necessary? Wouldn't it be a bit more lively if it went like this:

"Look, Joey, I don't care what you say, I'm not going in there."

"What are you talking about? You can't chicken out now."

"Do you know how long it's been since I've seen Sarah?"

"I don't know, ten, fifteen years?"

"She hates me, man. There's no way I'm going in there after what I did to her."

"Come on, Bobby, I'm sure she's past that already."

"What are you, nuts? I pretty much ruined her life. She'll probably spit in my face the minute she sees me."

"Don't be so dramatic."

"Dramatic? Do I look like someone who enjoys being humiliated?"

Breaking the dialogue up between two or more characters makes the scene much more dynamic and readable and keeps things moving. And notice how the same basic information is given, but some of it is coming out of Joey's mouth as well.

Next time you find yourself giving a character a long-winded speech, think about breaking it up.

You'll thank yourself later—and so will your readers.

APPROXIMATING REAL SPEECH

Dialogue is not and cannot be like real speech.

If you've ever listened to a recorded conversation you'll discover this very quickly. Years ago I used to transcribe police surveillance tapes for a lawyer and listening in on those conversations was an eye opener.

It took *forever* for anyone to get to the point, and often times they never did. Their exchanges were full of *ums* and *ahs* and half-completed sentences and thoughts. Frankly, it was a wonder any of the participants knew what they were talking about.

The dialogue in fiction is actually how we all *wish* we spoke. Complete sentences with complete thoughts.

You can, of course, break those up a bit, use interruptions, etc. to make it *appear* real, but all you're going for is the illusion of reality. Because reality itself is far too boring.

STAYING ON TRACK

Don't let your dialogue stray too far from the point of your scene.

Don't have your characters get lost in meaningless small talk—unless you've provided the subtext that moves the story forward through the emotion beneath that dialogue.

Dialogue is about moving the plot or characterization forward. Hopefully both.

KEEPING IT LIVELY

Here's a dialogue scene. Let me know what you think:

"Beautiful day, isn't it?"

"Oh, yes. Just lovely."

"Look at that sky. It's so blue. Sometimes I wish I could fly."

"I'm with you there. Flying would be so wonderful."

"The best."

"Yes, the best."

"That's what I love about you. You always agree with everything I say."

"And you with me. We make a great couple, don't we?"

Okay. Enough.

So now that you've read it, what's wrong with the above scene?

I think you already know. The last two lines of dialogue pretty much sum it up.

None of the dialogue in this scene tells us anything about these two people other than they're, quite possibly, the two most boring people on the face of the earth.

I could be wrong about that. At least they talk to each other.

But why are they boring?

Again, I'm starting to sound repetitive with some of these themes, but this is another point I feel needs to be hammered home.

Drama is about conflict.

And that doesn't only mean conflict in your plot, or conflict within a character, or conflict between two or more people, it also means conflict in the dialogue.

Much of this goes back to characterization. If these people have no conflict in their lives, their dialogue will surely be free of it, and those are not the kind of characters you want populating your story.

But even if you have two characters who generally agree with each other, there's no reason their dialogue has to be free of conflict.

How about this instead:

"Beautiful day, isn't it?"

"If you say so."

"Come on, just look at that sky. It's so blue. Makes me wish I could fly."

"You? Fly? You need three drinks before you'll even get on a plane."

"Yeah? Well, this is different. If I could sprout wings right now, I'd go for it."

"Uh-huh."

"That's what I love about you. You always agree with everything I say."

"And you with me. We make a great couple, don't we?"

Certainly the dynamics of the characterization and scene have changed, but in this case that's a good thing, right?

I sure think so.

Don't ever make it easy for your characters.

Even the most innocuous scene in the world can be made much more lively if you simply throw in a little conflict.

Try it sometime.

THE INDIRECT RESPONSE

One great way to keep your dialogue interesting is to use the indirect response.

When a character is asked a question, he or she doesn't respond directly, but how they *do* respond often tells us more about them.

For example:

He caught her at the front door. "You plan on stopping at Macy's?"

"I really do need something decent to wear. I'm almost ashamed to go outside."

"There's a liquor store right across the street from there. Can you pick me up a six pack?"

She looked at him. "Don't you think you've been drinking a little too much lately?"

"A couple beers aren't gonna kill me."

You'll notice in this exchange that not one of the questions asked is directly answered. The answer is implied, however, and the response tells us more about our characters than we might learn from a direct answer.

If you listen to real life conversation, you'll find that indirect responses are not uncommon. The next time you ask someone a question, listen carefully to what they say. Is it *really* an answer?

This technique is great for revealing character in a subtle, natural way.

THE REPEATER

This is a dialogue trick I find myself doing more than I should, but if used sparingly, it helps improve the flow:

Jenny frowned. "Why don't you just get off your butt and go to the store?"

"Go to the store?" he said. "Do I look like I have time for that? In case you haven't noticed, I've got a lot of work to do here."

Or...

"You're out of your mind, Sid. You're stone cold crazy."

"Crazy?" Sid cried. "What the hell are you talking about? I'm the only sane person in this room."

You get the idea. It's a very simple technique that can keep your readers reading.

DIALOGUE TAGS

This one's a real pet peeve of mine.

There's nothing that drives me nuts more in a novel than when an author uses a dialogue tag like this:

"I don't care what you think!" he exclaimed. "You can go to hell."

I once wrote a short suspense novel for a very well-regarded publishing house. After the book was written and I received the copy-edited manuscript, every single dialogue tag I'd written—every "said" or "asked"—had been changed to something like:

"Yes," she ejaculated;
"That's how I feel" he belched; and
"I don't believe that's true," she intoned.

Poke forks in my eyes right now.

Whoever this copy editor was—and if I knew, he or she might have a permanent limp right now—had decided that he/she did not like all of my boring old "saids" and decided to liven up my story with some more interesting dialogue tags.

I can't even begin to tell you how wrong this is. Wrong that a copy editor would take it upon himself to even make such changes, but also wrong, wrong, wrong, in terms of writing good fiction.

There are three dialogue tags you can use throughout your book that will never get you in trouble. Here's what they are:

Said.
Asked.
Told.

And here are more that you can get away with:

Shouted.
Called.
Moaned.
Murmured.
Muttered.
Groaned.
Cried.

There may be a few more, but your best bet is to use *all* of them sparingly, and stick to said and asked as much as possible.

Why?

Because the word said is pretty much invisible to the reader.

But having said that, I will go further to say that the less dialogue tags you use, the better.

The only reason they exist are:

1. To make it clear who's talking;
2. To alter the rhythm of the dialogue in order to make it flow better.

More often than not, it's simply better to write:

Kyle shook his head. "I don't think so."

Try reading the books of Ross MacDonald. Particularly the later Lew Archer stories. Check out the dialogue passages and you'll note that he rarely, if ever, uses dialogue tags. Yet we have no problem at all understanding who's talking.

Imagine that.

ACCENTS

Please don't do phonetic accents. They are too hard to read and come across stilted and weird. But if you absolutely must, do it *sparingly*.

The best way to approach an accent is to look at two things:

1. The structure of the sentence; and
2. Words or phrases that are common to the region the character originates from.

If you're character is foreign, for example, you'll find that, depending on which country she's from, the structure of her sentences is often different.

For an extreme example of this, just listen to the way Yoda speaks in the Star Wars movies:

"Go to him, you will."

A simple change of sentence structure can go a long way toward making the "accent" more convincing.

And sometimes simply *stating* that the character has an accent will plant that accent in the reader's mind and do much of the work for you.

19

Finding Your Voice

I can't tell you the number of times I've picked up a book that looked promising, only to discover after a few paragraphs that the prose was serviceable at best. And by serviceable, I mean that it got the job done, was not necessarily bad, but it simply had no... spark.

Try reading any book by Raymond Chandler and you'll see prose that has spark. Or Elmore Leonard, or Charles Portis, or Newton Thornburg, or my friends Cindy Gerard and Brett Battles and countless others.

They each have a voice that is unmistakable.

I mentioned this in an earlier chapter when I talked about Stephen King writing under the name Richard Bachman and my ability to spot King's work almost immediately. To readers paying attention, his voice sounds like no other.

Writing fiction isn't just a matter of telling a story. You need to tell that story with a style and confidence that separates you from the pack. You need to find your *own* voice.

And that can only be done after a lot of practice.

Most of us start out imitating our favorite writers. One of my favorites has always been William Goldman, and if you read my work, you'll certainly hear echoes of Goldman in it. But I like to think that I've moved beyond mere imitation and created something new. A voice that sounds like me and no one else.

I think finding your voice is as important to writing fiction as character, plot, story and dialogue. And I think that when readers like certain authors more than others, what they're reacting to is not simply the stories those authors tell, but the voice they use to tell them.

It has become painfully clear to me over the years, however, that some readers *don't* care about voice at all. But I don't think it's wise to use that fact as an excuse not to develop your own.

Never allow yourself to be satisfied with "serviceable" prose.

Work and keep working and polish your work until it shines like no other.

You'll be making the literary world a better place.

20

Show And Tell

I want to briefly speak about one of the most famous writing rules of all time. You hear teachers tell their students this. You see aspiring writers telling other aspiring writers that they need to follow this rule or no one will read their work:

Show Don't Tell.

While I understand the reasoning behind this rule, I just can't agree with it.

Why?

Because I'm a working writer and an active reader and the truth is that, while this is a nice rule of thumb, it isn't an unbreakable one. In fact, if you followed this rule all the time, I think it would render your story unreadable. Some of the examples I've seen used by others to demonstrate the concept to unsuspecting newbies were so strained they made my eyes roll.

To my mind, writing a story is closer to Show *and* Tell.

You show a little, you tell a little. You show a little more, you tell a little more.

In all honesty, I think that the *Show Don't Tell* rule ruins more aspiring writers than it helps. Too many of them take it far too literally.

So here's what I'm going to say about it—and I will undoubtedly get flack for saying this:

Ignore the rule.

Yes, I give you permission to never worry about showing versus telling again. Pick up any book and you'll see plenty of "telling." Because we are, after all, *telling a story*. You'll see a lot of showing as well.

The trick is to find a balance. And a good way to learn what the proper balance is, is to read widely and see how other authors balance their prose. Then to do a hell of a lot of writing until you find the proper balance that works for you.

You'll know it when readers start reacting favorably to your work.

So banish *Show Don't Tell* from your mind and think instead about Show *and* Tell.

It'll change your life.

21

Do I Need to Outline?

One question I always hear from aspiring writers is, "Do you outline your plots?"

Or the variation these days is "Are you a pantser or a plotter?"

(I've never understood that variation, really, because pantsers are plotters, too. They just do it on the fly.)

I remember asking the "Do you?" question myself a few times, back in the Stone Age when I was typing scripts and stories on my IBM Selectric.

If, by some weird stroke of fate, I happened to stumble across an honest to god real published writer (I didn't do conferences in those days, didn't know they existed, and there was no Internet— I'm *old*, okay?), the subject of outlining came up pretty quickly.

Why?

Because, like all aspiring writers, I was always searching for what works. A lot of us look at someone else's success and think, maybe I should do what they're doing. Human beings seem to have this unending desire to emulate others in hope that some of the fairy dust will rub off on us.

That would explain the thirty billion Star Wars clones that came out in the 1970's, and the gazillion comic book movies put into production after the Batman and Spider-Man and Iron Man franchises took off.

So when Bestselling Author X says he writes using an outline, it's only natural for aspiring writers to think that they need to outline, too.

I can guarantee you without a moment's hesitation that there are dozens, if not hundreds, of writing workshops going on in the world at this very moment where the workshop leader is telling his or her students to pull out the index cards and start mapping out their story.

And this is *not bad* advice.

The bad part is when they insist that this is the only way to properly construct a novel.

Because, the truth is, there is no one way to do anything in writing.

There is no single way to approach writing.

So in answer to the question that serves as a title for this chapter: *Do I Need to Outline?*

My response is, how the hell do I know?

Only you know if you need to outline. I don't care what anyone has told you, I don't care what their opinions might be concerning plot outlines—pro or con—it's entirely up to you to try it and discover whether or not it has a place in your writing process.

Certainly, if you've tried outlining and can't stand it, don't walk away feeling as if you're some kind of failure who will never write anything worth publishing.

That's nonsense.

Just because Jeffery Deaver writes really long outlines before he starts a book, and just because he writes great books that sell a zillion copies, does not mean that outlining is right for you (or that you'll sell even a dozen books).

Just because your university professor says the world will collapse if you don't outline, that doesn't mean it will. It won't.

Your professor may. But the world won't.

MY THOUGHTS ON OUTLINING

1. I hate it. If I outline, by the time I get to the actual writing itself, I feel as if I've already told the story. So my desire to flesh it all out has pretty much vanished. I'm not saying I can't do it. I'm not even saying I haven't done it when a contract required it. I just don't want to.

2. Did I mention that I hate it?

But that's just me. It might not be you. Here are some of the pros of writing an outline:

1. It'll keep you on track when you're writing the full draft. You won't get lost. You won't get stuck. All the hard plotting work will be done.

2. It'll...

Okay, I've run out of pros. And that's simply because I don't usually outline. Have no interest in it, thank you.

I write by the seat of my pants, always have, always will. The only exception I'll make is when I'm doing a book proposal and I have to write an outline (or at least a fully formed synopsis) to make the sale. Fortunately, now that I've gone indie, that doesn't really matter. I can write and publish whatever the heck I want.

But when I've *had* to outline, I did it. And I still hated it.

I'm a jump in and get to the writing kind of guy. And most of the writers I know take the same approach.

Doesn't mean they're right. Or wrong.

It just means they're plotting their stories the way that's most comfortable for them.

Which is what you should do, too.

And no matter which way you decide to go, don't ever, for even a minute, feel as if you're doing it wrong.

All that matters is what winds up on the page.

BUT, *WAIT*, WHAT IF I
WANT TO OUTLINE?
HOW DO I DO IT?

Honestly?

Every author does it differently. Some use those index cards. Some use the *What If* method I suggested in a previous chapter. Others just do quick bullet points that structure the story, or maybe write a line or two for each chapter.

If you want to know how *one* author does it, keep reading...

22

Sample Outline

I don't have an outline for any of my books except *The Paradise Prophecy*, which was required by my publisher and is *waaaaaaaaaay* too long and detailed to use here (seriously, it ran two hundred pages).

But the good news is that one of Braun Haus's new authors, Alana Matthews, creator of the *Parker & Coe, Love and Bullets* series, has graciously allowed me to include an outline she wrote for a romantic suspense novel.

Now, this is how *Alana* outlines. As always, it may or may not work for you.

BETRAYED

by Alana Matthews

We begin with Detective Jen Hunter getting her very first homicide call-out at three a.m. on a cold Saturday morning.

Doesn't matter, she's wide awake. Hasn't been able to sleep after news from her attorney that one of her ex-husband's motions in their court battle has been granted. They currently share custody of their four year-old daughter Megan, but Mickey—Jen's ex—is going after sole custody, claiming that because of the nature of her work, Jen is an unfit and inattentive parent.

This couldn't be more untrue, of course, but Jen worries that the court will see it Mickey's way and she'll lose Megan forever. It doesn't help that she's just been promoted and this is her first time up at bat.

Her supervisor, Bo Hendricks, hadn't scheduled her to report for duty until 9 AM Monday morning, but now she's been called out early and has no idea who her new partner will be.

The call-out doesn't take her far from home. A local Italian restaurant on The Hill has burnt down and investigators have found a partially burned body inside—a murder victim, shot to death. After dropping Megan off at Grandma Natalie's, Jen arrives at the scene, not surprised to find her brother Ryan running the arson investigation.

Turns out her new partner is an old college pal of Ryan's named Jack Landis. Landis took the fast track to the homicide squad and has been working cases for a couple years with great success. He recently received a promotion as well, to Detective First Grade, and was transferred to this district. So he and Jen are both new, in a way, and she hopes her knowledge of the area will gain her some brownie points as Landis shows her the ropes. Landis will be reporting her progress to Hendricks, and she wants high marks.

Despite her internal conflict over the custody battle—which she has done her best to set aside for the moment—Jen can't help brightening a bit when she sees Landis. With his blue eyes, and a hard body that no suit can disguise, Jack's a sight to behold.

As they all head into the crime scene, however, Ryan pulls his sister aside and says he noticed how she and Jack were scoping each other out, and advises her to stay away. It doesn't do to mix business with pleasure. Besides, Jack's a nice guy, but he's a "player," no better than her ex.

This should set off some alarms, but Jen figures it doesn't hurt to look, and the last person she's about to take relationship advice is from her brother. He's got a bit of a "player" reputation himself and his love life is a mess.

The body was found in the restaurant's walk-in freezer. Ryan tells them that whoever set the fire to try to cover the murder obviously didn't take the durability of the freezer unit into account, not to mention the observant neighbors who called 911 the moment they saw flames.

As a result, except for the bullet wound and a few minor burns, the victim escaped damage and is easily identifiable. Jen recognizes her immediately as Anita Campos, a neighborhood teenager who sometimes hung out with a group of punks who make the sidewalk in front of Gagglia's Grocery their home. The police are always chasing them away, but they come back like an army of ants. The punks have been busted for petty crimes, drug deals, and are suspected of a number of burglaries on The Hill.

Landis looks at the girl sadly—almost too sadly—and Jen senses that the sight of the body has stirred up some old memories for him. But before she can get up the nerve to ask him about it, he tells her they'll have to notify and interview the parents, and warns her that this is the toughest part of the job.

Taking Jen's car, they ride together to the Campos house and Jen volunteers to take the lead because she's part of the neighborhood. She's never had to make a death notification before and it is indeed one of the hardest things she's ever had to do. The look on Mr. and Mrs. Campos' faces—concern, astonishment, then deep, heart-wrenching grief—is one she'll remember for years to come.

The interview is rough going, but they manage to find out that Anita had been missing for a couple days, and get a name from Mrs. Campos: Anita's nineteen year-old boyfriend, Peter Breen, who they clearly disapproved of.

A lowlife who wasn't good for Anita.

With permission, they take a look at Anita's bedroom, Landis once again getting that look of sadness, and they find photos of Anita—a selfie using a pink cell phone, and several with a young man they assume is Peter Breen.

Mrs. Campos confirms it.

Landis suggests they check out Gagglia's Grocery, see if Breen's hanging with his buddies. Since it's only a block and a half away, they leave Jen's car where it's parked and go by foot. Along the way, they learn a little about each other. Landis is divorced, no kids, and struggling to figure out what to do with himself when he isn't working. His divorce is nearly two years old and he still hasn't gotten used to being alone.

Jen tells him about her own divorce and they immediately bond, Jen realizing that the attraction she felt earlier is beginning to grow. She's not a believer in love at first sight, but there's something about this guy that gets her motor running. She remembers her brother's warning, however, and pushes the feeling away, deciding that since this is her first time out as a homicide detective, she needs to remain professional at all times. The last thing she needs complicating her life right now is a relationship with a guy she barely knows. Especially when he's her partner.

Besides, cops and relationships are like oil and water.

When they get to Gagglia's Grocery, they spot two of the usual punks sitting on the curb out front. As they approach, however, one of the punks gets spooked and suddenly takes off running. No stranger to foot pursuits after years as a patrol officer, Jen sprints after him, nearly loses him, then finally tackles and cuffs him in an alleyway.

They show him the photograph of Breen and it takes some prodding (and a threat of arrest) to get the punk to admit he knows both Breen and Anita Campos. He even says he wouldn't be surprised if Breen killed Anita, considering she had recently dumped him. But when asked where Breen can be found, the punk has no idea. Breen hasn't been around the last couple days.

But as they leave the punk behind, a dark sedan rolls up next to him and a guy in sunglasses hands him an envelope.

"You did good," he says. "Played it exactly the way I told you to."

But when the punk eagerly opens the envelope, he finds it stuffed with blank paper. Before the punk can protest, Sunglasses pulls out a gun with a silencer and shoots him. Climbing out of his car, he grabs the body and unceremoniously tosses it in a nearby dumpster.

. . .

Over the next several hours, Jen and Landis work the case, using Breen's record of minor drug dealing convictions to guide them—offering Hendricks, their supervisor, updates along the way. They find out that Breen's last known address was an apartment across the city, but when they get there they discover the building has been abandoned. They take a look inside and find a number of drug addicts squatting there, and after a tense moment in the hallway—a potentially deadly encounter with one of the squatters —they decide that the trip is a bust and get out of there.

(It's during this encounter that Jen discovers Landis to be not only tough, but compassionate. These people aren't just human waste to him, but lost souls who need help. And his concern touches her. It reminds her of the compassion her father always shows to everyone around him. One of the things she loves most about Dad.)

Their next stop is Breen's parents' home, back on The Hill. It becomes obvious very quickly that they believe their son is something of a saint, and are completely unaware of his relationship with the dead girl. Or his involvement with drug dealers. They're convinced the police have the wrong Peter Breen, but photographs confirm that he's their man. The parents give them the same address that was listed in Breen's file, so if he isn't there, they have no idea where he might be.

But his little sister has a pretty good guess. She catches up to the detectives outside and says her parents have always been clueless, that Breen might be in one of the famed caves of St. Louis, which run under some of the city's neighborhoods—one of which is not that far from here. He and his sister found the place years ago and kept it a secret. Breen camps out there sometimes because he thinks it's "gangster."

He seemed nervous and scared the last time she saw him, and she's worried about him. She draws them a map to the entrance to the caves, but as they head out, Landis checks his rear view mirror and tells Jen they're being followed. This is the third time he's noticed the same late model sedan behind them—a guy wearing sunglasses at the wheel.

Landis makes an evasive maneuver and circles around behind the guy, then pulls him over. Jumping out of the car, he and Jen pull their weapons and confront the man—who it turns out is not the Sunglasses we met in the alley earlier, but somebody else altogether. He's a private detective, working for Jen's husband. He's been tasked to follow Jen around and photograph her activities for the custody case.

Incensed, Jen pulls the guy out of the car and is about ready to give him a beating, when Landis stops her and tells the guy to get lost. When he's gone, Jen rushes back to the car and breaks down.

"I feel like such a girl," she says to Landis, explaining the reason for the sudden breakdown—how she's afraid of losing her child—ashamed that she's allowing herself to cry when the job requires her to be tough and stable. But Landis assures her that gender has nothing to do with it. There isn't a man alive who doesn't cry once in a while and anyone who says he doesn't is a liar.

"Hell, after my divorce, I was a mess. Still am sometimes. And it was my idea."

He then tells her that one of the reasons for his divorce was because he wanted kids and she didn't. That he hopes one day to be a father, but won't hold his breath until it happens. Not at the rate he's going. So he fully understands her concern. No parent wants to lose what's most precious to them.

He gets that faraway look again, but shakes it off. And his willingness to listen and sympathize with Jen—even though they're virtual strangers—just makes him all the more attractive.

Where has this guy been all her life? If he's what her brother considers a "player," then sign her up for the next inning.

Or the whole game.

For a moment, as they sit there in the car, it seems as if the attraction is mutual, that they're just about to kiss, but the police radio squawks, cutting through the silence.

Remembering who she is and what they're supposed to be doing, Jen pulls herself together and promises she won't surprise Landis with any more breakdowns.

. . .

Jack, however, is struggling with his own feelings about Jen. She's beautiful, smart, and can handle herself in a tight situation. But it's more than that. There's something about her that's different than any woman he's ever known. He can't put his finger on what it is, but he knows he likes it. And in his mind's eye he can see himself making love to her...

But then this isn't time for school boy fantasies. They have work to do.

They follow the sister's map to the underground cave entrance —an old abandoned brewery just miles from The Hill. These underground caves are part of what makes St. Louis unique. The city was built atop a network of them, and a century or so ago, German brewers used them to house their beer, because of the natural cold air.

Now the caves are all but forgotten. Sealed off and buried in the history books. But every once in a while somebody stumbles upon an entranceway, and apparently one of those somebodies was Peter Breen.

It's late afternoon by the time they get to the abandoned brewery. The place hasn't seen business in a few decades and sits as a crumbling reminder of days gone by. Jen and Landis make their way past the chain link fence surrounding the place and go inside, following a set of stairs down to the basement, past faded signs that say STORAGE.

They find a reinforced door that's supposed to be locked, but the locks have been broken and it hangs ajar. After moving down another set up steps past chunks of crumbling cement, they find themselves in the dark network of caves. Jen flashes a light around and is surprised to find blood on the floor. Fresh blood.

They follow the tracks and find a smaller cave that has been set up as a hiding place—blankets, supplies, radio... And on the floor, his arm bleeding, is none other than Peter Breen. Breen stirs, sees them and pulls out a knife, brandishing it, obviously stoned, but scared out of his wits.

"I don't have it anymore," he slurs. "I got rid of it!"

It becomes clear that despite the fact that they're cops, Breen thinks they're here to kill him.

"Have what?" Jen asks.

"The cell phone," he tells her. "I dumped it. Nobody has to know. Nobody."

But when they start to question him, Breen's responses are borderline incoherent as he cries and raves on about Anita Campos. Landis takes an opportunity to snatch the knife away from him and they grab him, taking him back through the caves, up the stairs and out across the brewery grounds toward their car.

But as they're halfway there, still trying to question Breen, there's a change of pressure in the air and suddenly Breen's head snaps back, and he goes slack. They check him and discover that he's just taken a headshot—a sniper shot—and they dive, thinking they'll be next.

A moment later they hear the squealing of tires and look up to see a dark sedan beyond the fence, tearing down the street, too far away to get a tag number.

. . .

Their supervisor, Bo Hendricks, is incensed. He arrives at the scene in a mood, saying he shouldn't have put a rookie on this case, but he figured it would be routine. He was hoping his last few weeks before retirement would go smoothly, but now he has to clean up their mess.

He tells them that the body of Breen's friend—the guy they questioned near Gagglia's Grocery—has been found in a dumpster, and it's obvious to Jen that they were set up. The killer used them to help him track Breen down, and they led him straight to the guy.

They tell Hendricks about Breen's ramblings. Something about a cell phone. That he was terrified of them, but never quite told them why. Hendricks asks if they found this alleged cell phone, but Breen claimed to have gotten rid of it. Even so, it may be in the caves somewhere.

Hendricks nods, saying this is obviously a professional hit. He thinks the phone may be key here, and says he's now officially taking the lead on the case. He'll supervise the search of the caves, while they handle the family notification and follow up with Breen's sister.

Jen isn't thrilled about having to make another notification and lets Landis take the lead this time. When they question Breen's sister, she says her brother didn't have a cell phone anymore, but was always borrowing Anita's. It must be her phone they're looking for.

They check with Mr. and Mrs. Campos, again searching Anita's room, but no phone is found. Landis once again has that faraway look in his eyes when he sees the girl's photo, and when they get back to the car, Jen finally asks him about it.

He tells her that Anita reminds him of his older sister, who was murdered when he was thirteen years old. He remembers the cops coming to their house, his mother in hysterics, his father crying, the pall that hung over their household for months afterward. They never found the killer and Jack vowed at the age of twelve that he'd become a cop one day and find the guy himself. It was crazy kid thinking, but he at least followed through on the first part. And he does look through her file once in a while to see if there's anything the original investigators may have missed.

Jen sympathizes, attracted to his vulnerability, and suddenly they're kissing, right there in the car. It's a mistake—and they both know it—but that doesn't stop them, and Jack's kiss is like nothing she's ever experienced before. Sends a stutter of electricity through her body like no other.

They both pull away, embarrassed by this lapse, and awkwardly report into Hendricks about their progress on the case. He tells them he'll handle things from here on out and they can call it night.

Jen and Landis look at each other, then Jen goes against her better judgment and mentions that they're close to her house— does he want to come over for a while to decompress after a long day?

After only a moment's hesitation, he agrees, and Jen calls Grandma Natalie to explain that she'll be a little late in picking up Megan.

The moment the door closes behind them, they attack each other in Jen's living room, the pent up passion overwhelming them. Then the blinds are quickly drawn and they're soon making love on the couch.

But what they don't realize is that there's a figure in the shadows on Jen's front porch, camera pressed against the window, finding a view through a tiny crack in the blinds, clicking away, recording this moment of passion.

It's the private detective hired by Jen's ex-husband...

. . .

The next morning, Jack Landis is asleep in his own bedroom when the phone rings. It's Jen. She's taking Megan to church and afterward they're getting together at Grandma Natalie's house for a meal. Does he want to join them?

Landis would like nothing more, but doesn't want to sound too anxious, so he hesitates. Then Jen reminds him that he said he doesn't know what to do with himself when he's alone—so this is his chance to do something.

Jack soon discovers that having a meal with the family Hunter is a bit like riding a roller coaster. The food is amazing, the company excellent (including Ryan, Jonathan, Grandma Natalie and Jen's dad, Marty Hunter), but the good-natured spats between siblings and cousins and aunts and uncles make Landis feel a bit awkward.

The one true joy Landis discovers, however, is Megan. He takes to her immediately, and Jen is both touched and thrilled by this.

But then Ryan pulls her aside, says he can see that something's going on between them and chastises her for ignoring his warning. Soon little brother Jonathan gets in on the conversation, telling Ryan to leave her alone—she's a grown up—and in the middle of an increasingly heated argument, Jen gets a phone call.

Excusing herself, she takes it, surprised to find it's the private detective her ex hired to follow her. He wants to meet, promising Jen it'll be worth her while. Jen reluctantly agrees, tells everyone she'll be right back, and meets the guy at a nearby park.

The PI holds out his camera, showing her one of the photographs he took of her and Landis on her living room couch. Says if she doesn't want them going to her ex, she'd better pay up.

But Jen isn't about to take any b.s. from this guy. Knocking him down, she takes the camera away from him and starts clicking through the photos, erasing each one. The PI tells her she's wasting her time—he has copies—but she's suddenly found something else of interest and isn't listening to him.

A photograph has caught her attention: a shot of Jen and Jack going into the brewery. The photo is taken from a distance with a telephoto lens, but in the corner of the frame is a parked sedan— the very sedan they saw squealing away after Breen was shot. The license plate number is clearly visible.

Excited, she leaves the PI on the ground and goes back to her car, calling in the plate number, and soon discovers that it belongs to a former cop she knows by reputation—the very cop she replaced on the homicide squad, Charlie Coe, who is now running private security for the mayor. Coe also happens to be the best friend of her boss, Bo Hendricks.

Thinking about the cell phone Breen was babbling about, Jen goes to Landis and tells her what she's found and the two wonder what their boss's involvement in this is. He seemed awfully anxious to take over the case and find that phone.

Together, they break into Hendricks's office, jimmy open his desk and find a blue cell phone in a plastic bag. Thinking back to the selfie they saw of Anita in her bedroom, they know they have what Breen claimed to have gotten rid of. Checking the files, they find that the internal disk has been erased.

But all is not lost, Jen says, and they take the phone to her younger brother Jonathan, who's a deputy for the Sheriff's department. He sends them to their best computer forensic tech, who retrieves the lost files.

Moments later, they sit in their car watching an extended video of the mayor making a pay-off to a notorious local gangster, followed by footage of Charlie Coe and Bo Hendricks coming toward the camera, guns drawn.

They can only conclude that Hendricks, who is about to retire, plans to join Coe as private security for the mayor, who is obviously dirty. And the clean-up of the mess meant killing Anita Campos and Peter Breen. Breen must have gotten away with the cell phone, so they put Plan B into action.

Charlie Coe confirms this a moment later. His gun trained on them, he hops in the back seat, calls Hendricks and tells him to meet them at the abandoned brewery. He then forces Jen to drive there with plans to dispose of the two detectives in the caves.

It'll be years before anyone finds them.

Hendricks is waiting for them when they get there. But just when things look dire, Jack manages to overpower Coe, and after a deadly cat-and-mouse chase through the caves, Jen and Jack are triumphant—killing Coe in self-defense and wounding Hendricks, who they immediately cuff and book for murder.

In the days that follow, Jen and Landis find themselves falling hopelessly in love and destined to get married, as the Hunter family brothers secretly pay a visit to Jen's ex advising him to withdraw his custody suit and stick to the current arrangement. Otherwise he'll find himself with closer family ties than he either needs or wants.

Jen isn't sure why her ex suddenly had a change of heart, but she doesn't question it, and looks forward to the years ahead when she and Megan and Jack can make a home together.

THE END

Thank you, Alana.

Notice how she gets the tone of the piece down as well as the basic plot beats, structure and character motivations? And she does it all in a few pages.

Now when she sits down to write, she knows exactly where she's going and doesn't have to think too hard. Even if she strays from this outline, she always has a place to come back to.

Does this make me want to outline?

No.

But if I were going to do it, this is exactly how I would.

23

Do I Need to Research?

A few years back, I was stuck on a story point.

I was working on my latest novel, a thriller, and I had a guy trapped in the trunk of his car and I wasn't sure how to get him out.

It seems like an easy enough thing, getting a guy out of a trunk, but this particular guy was bound and gagged and so cramped he could barely move.

But that wasn't why I was having trouble. My problem was that I had him trapped in the trunk of a Toyota Corolla, but I don't have a Corolla—especially a ten year old model—and I had absolutely no idea whether a ten year old Corolla has a trunk release.

So what did I do?

A couple of things. First, I got online and looked up as much about Toyota Corollas that I could find. I managed to put in a search term for trunk releases and ten-year old Toyotas and actually found a website that helped me.

The second thing I did was contact an author friend of mine who drives a Toyota and asked him to check out his trunk. Well, he went a step further and actually locked himself inside his own trunk and tried to get out.

That's above and beyond.

All of this for a simple task of helping a character escape from a trunk. After a bit of research, I was no longer stuck and continued buzzing along happily with the story.

But here's the thing:

I'm not a big fan of research. When I'm ready to write, I'm ready to write and researching a subject is the last thing on my mind. So

I tend to just sit down and start writing and worry about researching a fact only when it's absolutely necessary.

If I come across something I need help with, a simple flip of the screen to Google helps me find just about anything I need. I always make sure, however, that I go to more than one source for the information—usually several—just to make sure it's accurate.

A filmmaker by the name of Jake Kasdan did a great little movie called *Zero Effect* about a wacky detective investigating a murder. During the course of his investigation, the detective—played by Bill Pullman—gives his partner (Ben Stiller) a tidbit of information about motel room mattresses that turns out to be fairly important to the plot.

Well, if you listen to the commentary track on the DVD, it turns out that Kasdan made it all up.

Now, I imagine there must be a mattress manufacturer or salesman out there would look at the movie and say, "that's complete baloney."

But does it really matter?

For most of us, Kasdan gets away with it and our suspension of disbelief remains intact.

The key to writing and research is to keep it plausible. If something sounds to the average reader as if it could be reasonably true, then I think you're okay.

But you do have to be careful. There are certain subjects—like guns, for instance—that readers tend to be real sticklers about. There are also authors out there who meticulously research every minute detail of their books.

I know of one writer who often spends months visiting the locales of the book he wants to write, not putting a word to paper until he has soaked in every last detail of the place, sometimes at the expense of actually sitting down and writing.

But you know what? He writes amazing books. And I can imagine the people who live in the cities he researches would swear he's a native.

If you want to do that, fine. I'd rather jump in and start writing and fill in the details as I go. My goal is to stay true to my characters and create a plausible world for them to inhabit.

I probably shouldn't admit this, but I wrote the book *Kiss Her*

Goodbye and set it in Chicago long before I ever visited the city. I've since been there and fallen in love with the place (and set my *Trial Junkies* books there as well), but before then I had to fake it.

And you know what?

The director who adapted and directed the TV version of *Kiss* said to me that I really captured the city well. I didn't dare tell him I had only relied on the Internet and questions to friends who live there to make it authentic.

The trick, I've found, is to sprinkle in a detail here and there and then lie with confidence.

There's also the danger of over researching. If you have all those facts floating around in your head, you tend to want to show off your knowledge, and you forget that you're telling a story. Facts are fun, but if they bog the story down, get rid of them. Throw them out.

So the bottom line here is that research is good, but it's okay to make stuff up as well, as long as you don't get caught.

After all, that's why they call it fiction.

24

Will I Need an Agent?

The next two chapters go a bit beyond the nuts and bolts of writing, but I wanted to include them because I know so many of you want to know the answer to the above question.

So, here we go.

The short answer, in the days of indie author entrepreneurship is...

That depends

Back in the Stone Age (somewhere around 2010 or so), just about the *only* way you could get your book to a major publisher was through an agent. Actually, that's still true today, but those of us who have gone indie don't need a major publisher. Or a publisher at all, for that matter.

So it all depends on how you plan to publish.

Agents became a thing because publishers got tired of rummaging through their slush pile of submitted manuscripts, looking for publishable work. I don't know the history here, but I can imagine that the first agents were likely former publishing house employees—editors or sales staff—who already had relationships with a number of editors around town.

They developed those relationships and said, "Hey, I'll go through that slush pile for you and it won't cost you a cent."

"How are you going to make a living?" asked the harried and skeptical editor.

"Easy," the agent told him. "I'll charge the author a percentage of his royalties."

The editor smiled. "I think I like that idea. Win-win."

Okay, I can't be sure it went down like that, but like all middle men, these guys are looking to make and save money, and in traditional publishing that usually comes at the expense of the author. That isn't bitterness talking, merely fact.

Let's be real here. You're basically paying an agent 15% of your royalties so he or she will send your manuscript to a bunch of editors he knows and hopes one of them will bite. And since most publishers have closed their doors to "unsolicited submissions," you have no choice but to play the game.

But let's not forget that agents also negotiate the deal, if you manage to get one. Agents who know their way around a contract and can negotiate a good one are invaluable to an author seeking traditional publication.

If you've chosen to go indie, you don't have a deal to negotiate. If your plan is to hire an editor and cover artist and possibly a formatter and pay them a fixed cost for their services rather than give up the majority percentage of your sales, then *no*, you don't need an agent.

OKAY, BUT WHAT ABOUT FOREIGN RIGHTS? DON'T I NEED AN AGENT FOR THAT?

We're getting closer and closer to the point where we don't even need agents for foreign deals anymore. A lot of indies are striking their own deals or hiring their own translators or going through Amazon Crossing.

After I wrote *Trial Junkies*, Amazon came to me and offered to publish the book in both German and French. And the biggest foreign market (for U.S. authors, that is) is the UK, and since most of us write our books in English, we don't need translations or UK publishers, so no need for an agent to sell the UK rights.

WHAT ABOUT MOVIES AND TV?

Want to know how I sold *Kiss Her Goodbye* to Sony Television? My agent at the time sure didn't do it.

No, the producer read a short story of mine in an anthology and liked it enough to try one of my novels. He liked that one even better, then contacted my agent to see if the rights for both were available.

Now, trust me, if you find yourself in that position, you definitely want an agent to handle the negotiations with Hollywood. But do you know what my book agent did?

He tossed the ball to an actual Hollywood film and TV agency (*CAA*) and *they* negotiated the deal with the production company.

So my advice for that movie and TV deal? You'll need someone whose sole purpose is to get your work in front of Hollywood producers. Get a movie and TV agent.

Of course, that's a whole different ballgame that isn't easy to play, and you will likely find yourself on the query treadmill for awhile before you find one. And there's every possibility that a literary agent can help connect you with a Hollywood agency as mine did. That said, remember that you're giving up a percentage of your book sales *and* your movie/TV sales in the process.

It may be well worth it for you. Or it may not. Only you can decide.

WHAT IF I REALLY *DO* WANT TO GO TRAD PUB?

Okay, I know some of you really want that publishing deal. And that's fine. And, yes, you *will* need an agent to do it.

So how do you get one?

Many agents get their clients through referral. One of their writers or friends or associates says, "Hey, I just read this great manuscript and you've definitely got to take this guy (or girl) on."

And that's a sure way to get your book moved to the top of the reading pile.

SO HOW THE HECK DO YOU GET SOMEONE TO GIVE YOU A REFERRAL?

I'm afraid it's going to cost you money.

No, this isn't an agent referral scam. Calm down.

I don't want any more money from you (although I won't argue if you feel compelled to buy another one of my books—they make great gifts).

One of the best ways to get a referral is through networking.

Now, you can try to do that networking online, which will cost you practically nothing. Make friends with writers and agents through their blogs, their Facebook pages, through Twitter, what have you.

But such an approach can be problematic. Mostly because professionals are always a bit wary of people who hit them up to read their manuscript.

So what you really need to do is spend some money and get your butt to one of the many writers' conferences that are held every year throughout the country. These conferences include Bouchercon, Thrillerfest, Left Coast Crime, RWA, and the Romantic Times Booklovers Convention.

The beauty of these conferences is that you are surrounded by people who are actively working in the publishing industry. Agents, editors, publishers, writers, booksellers, and librarians.

There isn't much a bookseller or librarian can do for you at this stage of your career, but if you make your presence known with the agents, editors, publishers and writers—introduce yourself and buy them a drink, get to know them on a personal level—then your chances of getting that referral will raise accordingly.

The last thing you want to do is come on too strong. You don't just walk up to a guy and say, "Hey, will you read my book?"

He or she is likely to smile politely, then run in the opposite direction. But if you can have a genuine conversation with one of these people, and find a way to weave your pitch into that conversation, then you may well find yourself faced with an opportunity to get your work read.

Another great thing about many of the conferences is that they often have workshops and pitch fests that you can attend that will put you face to face with these very same professionals. In these pitch fests, you will be given a few minutes to talk to an editor or an agent, and if they like your pitch, they may well request a partial or even full manuscript.

The Romantic Times Booklovers Conference is especially good for this—assuming you write romantic fiction (although they're starting to branch out a bit, which is why I've attended to promote my thrillers). They devote an entire wing of the conference to aspiring writers, and one I spoke to told me she had been asked by several different editors for a partial manuscript.

But even if you don't do a pitch session, you will be meeting a ton of people at these conferences, all of them either professionals or aspiring writers like yourself. Today's aspiring writer is tomorrow's pro, so you never know when these friendships will pay off.

But I can say for a fact that they do work.

Over the years I have referred people I met on the conference circuit to my former agent. We struck up a friendship, they sent me their work, and I was impressed enough to send that work on.

And I know several other writers who got their agent the very same way.

Short of that, you can send out query letters or emails that may or may not be read. I have a friend who went that route and got a very good agent that way.

But, if you're sticking to the indie world, why bother?

Why pay another middle man to do what you can easily do on your own?

That said, if you *do* decide to look for an agent, you'll need to know how to pitch your story when you're in that conference bar, so keep reading to find out how...

25

If You Do Want An Agent...

What you're about to read is an article I wrote many years ago in an attempt to help aspiring writers develop their elevator pitch to use when trying to find an agent. This will be important to those of you who *do* want an agent, so pay close attention.

But there's another reason you might want to read as well.

If you're an indie author, it may help you write your cover copy. And knowing how to write cover copy is all important.

So I think this article—as dated as it might be in some respects—is still useful in teaching you how to cut your storyline down to its bare essence.

ANATOMY OF A LOGLINE

You've written your book. You've labored over it for months or years and polished every syllable until your masterpiece is ready to hit the marketplace. Now comes the hard part: finding someone —preferably an agent—to read it.

"Find" is actually the wrong word. What you really have to do is *attract* readers. And to attract readers you have to call on all your skills as a salesman.

"Salesman?" you cry. "I'm a writer not a salesman!"

Uh-huh. Glad you've enjoyed your stint in fantasyland, my friend, but it's time to take a step into the real world.

At this point, you have a product that needs to be moved and there's only one way to move it: Advertising. Any good salesman knows all about the benefits of advertising. From the biggest corporation with their multi-million dollar commercials to the guy standing on the street holding a sign for the local car dealer: *Big Savings! Today Only!*

Advertising is what any good salesman uses to attract buyers. You go to a used car dealer to see what's available and what happens? The salesman comes over and guides you toward the latest lemon while he tries to smooth-talk you into buying it. And, boy does he make it attractive. It has the latest this and the latest that and it's only been driven by a little old lady on weekends, and this baby purrs. His sales pitch is his advertisement.

And that's exactly how you get people to read your book. Your sales pitch. You have to prepare your pitch both verbally and on paper and you have to present it with confidence and polish.

You've all probably heard of a Svengali Deck, otherwise known as TV Magic Cards. For those of you who haven't, a Svengali Deck is a special deck of playing cards that allows the user to perform a dozen or more amazing card tricks without having to develop any sleight-of-hand skills.

In the old days, magician/pitch-men used to stand on street corners or at swap meet booths and demonstrate the wonders of this deck of cards by showing you an eye-popping trick. This trick would be brief and straight to the point—just enough to show off the virtues of the deck and get you digging for the cash to buy one.

When you prepare your all-important sales pitch to entice readers to your book, you have to approach it with the same economy and magic the magician/pitch-men use. You have to get your story across in a few simple words and those words must have eye-popping appeal. They must have that wow quality that forces the reader to say, "I've gotta read that!"

That's where your logline comes in.

A logline is a one or two-sentence summary of your story. Probably the best place to find a sample logline is to look in your TV Guide or local equivalent, which are full of brief story summaries. But let me give you an example.

Since I come from a screenwriting background, where loglines are as common as beautiful young starlets, let's take a look at a movie logline:

After he's wrongly convicted of murdering his wife, a high-powered surgeon escapes custody and hunts down the real killer, a one-armed man.

This, of course, is from *The Fugitive.* Maybe not the liveliest logline in the world, but it tells you just about everything you need to know about the movie. We know who the lead character is, what his dilemma is and, most importantly, what he hopes to accomplish.

What we have above is essentially the spine of the story— the sentence the entire movie hangs on. Sure, we could talk about the relentless U.S. Marshal who is after the doctor; we could talk about the train crash and the chase sequences and the experimental liver drug, but when it comes to the logline, none of that really matters. We don't have time for it.

Like that TV Magic card trick, your logline has to be simple and to the point and it has to attract the reader to the possibility of a great read. When I look at the above logline, I think, 'Wow, that sounds like it could be an exciting story."

And, of course, we all know it is.

The anatomy of a logline is this: The lead character has a problem and must achieve a certain goal in order to solve that problem. Who, What, How. *Who* is the lead character, *what* is his problem and *how* is he going to solve it.

Let's take a look at *The Fugitive* again:

Who: *A high-powered surgeon.*
What: *Wrongly convicted of murdering his wife.*
How: *He escapes custody to hunt down the real killer.*

Chances are pretty good that you're scratching your head right now and saying, "But my story is much too complex for that."

This may be true, but when you're at a conference trying to convince someone to read your book, you don't have time for much detail. At least not for that initial grab.

After you have their attention, then you can launch into a slightly more complex version that really sells the book.

Let's take a look at a fairly complex story: *The Godfather.*

We all know The Godfather is full of vivid characters and great subplots and big moments, but what really is the essence of the story?

Here's what I get:

When his father is gunned down, a gangster's "good" son must reluctantly seek revenge and take over the family business.

Who: *A gangster's son*
What: *His father is shot.*
How: *He seeks revenge and takes over the family business.*

The story plays on a rich canvas, but it is much less about Vito Corleone, the Godfather, and more about Michael, the up and coming Godfather. It is the story of his ascent (or descent, depending on your POV) to the leadership of the Family. Much of the story leads up to the moment Vito Corleone is shot, then follows Michael as he gets revenge and eventually takes over as head of the organization. Everything in the story hangs on that simple logline or spine.

If you follow the usual marketing strategies, you'll be sending out query letters and making phone calls and throwing your pitch at just about everyone in your path.

A really concise, well thought out logline will help you get the results you want.

TECHNIQUES IN ACTION

Wherein Rob gives you an actual example
of these tips and tricks in action.

26

So What Have We Learned?

Before I let you go on your way, let's take a moment to look at some of the key points I've made.

Here are the headline versions:

Keep it simple. Keep it direct. Keep it clear.

When creating your characters, remember attitude, emotion, goal and action.

Writing a story is like building a house. Without a solid foundation, it's bound to fall apart.

Any good story should have rhythm, aided by the ebb and flow of your scenes.

Conflict is essential, even in the most innocuous of scenes.

Get in, make your point, then get the heck out.

Find your subplots organically. Don't tack them on for the sake of filling out the story.

Don't be afraid to make readers do some work. Let them read between the lines rather than slap them in the face.

*Dialogue is an **approximation** of real speech. It's how we wish* *we really spoke.*

Practice, practice, practice.

Keep working until you find your voice and make it sing.

Stop aspiring and start perspiring.

These "rules" seem to work for me.

I hope you'll get some value out of them, too, but as I said at the beginning, use what works for you and discard the rest. We all have to discover what works best for us and not worry too much about what other writers are doing.

Before we're done, however, I feel I should put up or shut up. I find that in most books on craft, the authors may include snippets of prose (as I have), but rarely offer up a complete manuscript with a beginning, middle and end.

So as a bonus, what follows is my novella, *Side Steal* (aka *Flight 12*).

Some of you may have read it (it's currently available on Amazon), but I urge you to read it again while keeping in mind the things I've talked about here.

Then you can point at me and say, "Hey, you broke your own rules!"

And chances are I have.

Thank you for reading...

Side Steal

A Nick Jennings Thriller

Robert Gregory Browne

1

Jennings was in the middle of a hand when his phone rang.

The first few bars of *She Blinded Me With Science* blasted out of his coat pocket, looping interminably as it sliced through the silence and provoked looks of contempt from the other players.

He was down to his last nickel, holding only a pair of deuces, and knew he was in serious trouble. He had hoped to hell he could bluff his way out of this hole or he'd go home with a big fat zero. Not the way he wanted to end the night.

But the phone continued to bray, so he pulled it out of his pocket, intending to kill it before the next loop. Then he saw the name on the screen—

Cassandra.

He hadn't heard from Cassie in months, and she wasn't the type to call him for no good reason. She had been largely hands off since the divorce, a decision he wasn't in a position to argue with.

She had a reputation to protect.

Jennings looked at the deuces, then at the table full of increasingly annoyed players, then at the phone, then at the deuces again.

Tossing the sorry mess into the muck, he said, "I'm out."

Someone muttered, "In more ways than one, you don't kill that friggin' noise."

Jennings ignored him, got to his feet, and pushed his way outside. The Vegas night air hit him like a blast of exhaust from an idling semi-truck. He sometimes wondered why he tolerated it. Why he didn't move to Northern California or even Hawaii, where the weather was a lot kinder and the lifestyle a little more relaxed.

But Jennings was Vegas born and bred. He couldn't imagine living anywhere else. It was home and always would be—flaws and all.

As the door to the Jolly Aces Poker Lounge swung closed behind him, he finally answered the phone. "Hey, kid. This is a surprise."

"For both of us," Cassie said. "I have a favor to ask and you know how I hate asking favors."

"Especially from me."

"Let's not turn this into a soap opera, all right?"

"I think the last time I heard from you was back in April, and I'm pretty sure you were a little drunk. You kept trying to pick a fight and when I wouldn't take the bait you got pissed and finally—"

"I apologized for that," she said.

"Yeah, there's nothing more personal than an email."

Cassie sighed. Her sighs were usually abrupt and full of scorn, but Jennings sensed a trace of embarrassment in this one. Or maybe he was imagining things. "I was having a rough time of it that week, okay? I can't be super cop all the time."

"Nobody expects you to be. Least of all me."

"Anyway, we're getting off subject here."

"I didn't know we were ever *on* subject."

"Quit trying to be cute, Nick. I'm immune to it and it doesn't suit you. The reason I called is to ask you to speak to a friend of mine."

Jennings paused. "About?"

"Some work she needs done."

"What kind of work?"

"Off the books stuff. But it's better you hear it from her than me. I've already been told to back burner the case and the farther away I stay from it the better. My captain says I'm too emotionally involved."

"Wait a minute. You have a friend involved in one of your cases? What are you trying to get me into?"

"Not really a friend," she said. "Her name is Rachel Brennan and she'll tell you all about it. But don't worry, I didn't promise her anything. She knows you've got the skills, but I didn't guarantee you'd take her on."

"Well thank God for that. What does she need?"

"Help finding someone she lost."

"A missing persons gig?"

"Just talk to her, okay? I know you can't be getting much satisfaction showing card tricks to a room full of drunk tourists, so maybe helping someone who needs it might help *you* recalibrate your life. Do something worthwhile for a change."

"You don't think much of me, do you?"

"Don't start, Nick. We've been down that road more times than I care to remember and it still has all the same potholes. Just meet with her. If you don't like what she has to say, walk away."

"Cass, I don't know what you're expecting from me, but the last time I tried to flex my muscles you told me there's nothing worse than an ex-cop on a mission. And unless you manage to pull a P.I. license out of that cute little butt of yours, I've got no authority to do much of—"

"Rachel Brennan," Cassie said. "She'll be at the Four Jacks lounge at eleven p.m."

Then the line went dead.

Jennings had no intention of going to the Four Jacks.

The game he'd just walked out on had started at two that afternoon and he'd lost most of his rent. He needed to track down Scully and start thinking about possible money-making opportunities.

Scully was a two-bit con artist and sometime cat burglar Jennings had met when he was still a cop. Picked him up on a B&E late one night. Caught him strolling nonchalantly out of the front door of a pink stucco townhome in Paradise Palms, a sack full of goods in hand. Jennings knew a perp when he saw one and immediately pulled over and commanded him to halt.

Scully didn't resist. Offered Jennings a shrug and said, "This can't be anything but fate. Nobody has luck this bad."

During the ride into the station, Jennings and Scully struck up a conversation and despite himself, Jennings found he liked the little guy. It almost hurt to take him into central booking, but he was a straight cop and did what he pledged to do.

Months later, after his spectacular fall from grace, Jennings found himself divorced, broke, and in need of some work. So he brushed off the old card magic act he'd once performed as a teenager and started hitting the local bars in hopes of scoring a magic bartender gig.

One of those bars was the Pin Drop Lounge at the Golden Sands Bowling Alley. The first person he saw when he stepped through the doors was Scully, at a table in a corner, nursing a beer and studying a daily racing form with the intensity of a college student cramming for finals. On impulse, Jennings walked over.

"Contemplating your next crime spree?"

Scully looked up sharply, did a bit of a double take, then greeted him with a big smile. "Well, well, if it ain't the guy who almost landed me in the bucket."

"Almost?"

He shrugged. "My attorney can talk a monkey into giving up his bananas. You ever need his name, just let me know."

"If he's anything like my divorce lawyer, I think I'll pass."

"Divorce, huh?" Scully studied him. "I take it the wound's pretty recent. You *are* looking a little raw. You want a beer?"

Jennings decided why not? It wasn't like he was a cop anymore, so what did it hurt to share a beer with a known but likable felon?

"Sure," he said and pulled up a chair.

Before the night was over, the two were fast friends and had been hanging together ever since. And sometimes, in an attempt to supplement their meager incomes, they worked together, too.

Scully was a very good teacher.

Now, since much of *Jennings's* income was sitting on a green felt table, it only made sense to see what Scully might have lined up for them. But as he climbed into his recently salvaged Crown Vic, he thought about Cassie and what she'd think of him if he failed to meet up with this Rachel Brennan.

Because despite everything they'd been through, he still cared about Cassie.

He always would.

There were even nights he'd lay in bed, staring at the cracked ceiling of his apartment, wishing he could find a way to make her see him again. To make her look past the grief they shared and remember the man he'd once been.

So he fired up the Vic and started driving, and fifteen minutes later he parked in the lot of the Four Jacks Hotel & Casino and sat drumming his fingers on the steering wheel, knowing he was about to be sorry.

Then he sighed and forced himself out of his car, walked into the cool, smoky air of the casino, and wound his way through the clanging slot machines toward the Big 8 Lounge.

Sorry would turn out to be the least of his worries.

He should have been watching for land mines.

3

A band played Motown funk on the lounge stage. Four middle-aged black guys in red, shiny bell bottomed jumpsuits, backing a spandexed blonde beauty queen with a voice as loud and shrill as the casino she worked in.

Whoever had chosen this place for a meeting clearly hadn't thought it through.

As Jennings stepped inside, it occurred to him that he had no idea what Rachel Brennan looked like. Cassie hadn't bothered to tell him. He glanced around the darkened room, saw that there were any number of possibilities sitting at the small tables clustered around a minuscule—and mostly empty—dance floor. But none of them gave him a second look.

Jennings checked his watch, saw that he was five minutes early, then crossed to a booth in back and slid in.

The assault on his ears was relentless; one more reason to regret his decision to come here. He decided to order a drink, and if this Rachel person didn't find him in the amount of time it took him to slap it down (assuming Cassie hadn't neglected to describe *him* to her), he'd bag out of here and go find Scully.

But before he could signal a waitress, a Keno girl in a short black skirt and a Four Jacks vest made her way past the cluster of tables and came over to him.

He was about to wave her away when she said, "Mr. Jennings?"

She sounded young—barely into her twenties, maybe—but her face was shadowed and all he could really see were her startling blue eyes, which were almost phosphorescent in the darkness of the lounge.

"Ms. Brennan?"

"The one and only," she said. "Around here, at least. But I've got some bets to run and I wanted to introduce myself so you wouldn't think I was a no-show. The band'll be taking a break after the next song, and we'll be able to talk then."

As if on cue, a flash of cheap pyrotechnics shot from the stage and the lounge briefly lit up, giving Jennings a clearer look at her face. And the moment he saw it, his stomach dropped. All at once he knew why Cassie had wanted him to come here. And why her captain had said she was too emotionally involved.

Rachel Brennan had their daughter's face.

His and Cassie's.

In fact, in a different world, she could have been Michelle's older sister.

"Mr. Jennings?"

He struggled to find his voice. "Just call me Nick."

"Are you okay? You look like you could use a drink."

He thought he might like several at the moment. The memories were rearing up on him with brutal clarity.

"I'm fine," he said. "Go do your job."

She nodded and turned and crossed toward the Keno station just outside the lounge, the image of her face—of Michelle's face—lingering in the darkness where she had stood.

Jennings closed his eyes, trying to push back the pain as he remembered an empty bedroom, a desperate search, and the phone call that had ended it all. His life and his career. A phone call that told him his daughter, his beautiful fourteen-year-old girl, had been found raped and strangled and left to die in a Boulder City drainage ditch.

They'd lost their baby girl four years ago. And if Michelle were still alive, she'd be close to Rachel Brennan's age.

Jennings got to his feet, headed out of the lounge and into the casino, losing himself for a moment amid the flashing lights and the *ring ding clang* of the slots. Then he pushed his way outside, yanked out his phone and hit speed dial.

Cassie answered on the second ring.

"Fuck you," he said.

She was silent for a long moment. "I wasn't expecting this call so soon."

"You couldn't have warned me? You had to blind side me like this? Jesus, Cassie, your captain is right about you."

"I'm sorry, Nick, but I thought if you saw her you'd understand why I wanted you to meet her."

"She isn't Michelle."

"You think I don't know that? But she could be. She could be our little girl desperately looking for someone to help her when nobody will. Have you even talked to her yet?"

"Long enough to say hello."

"So... what? You just walked out on her?"

"She's working. We're supposed to do a sit down in a couple minutes."

"And you're already halfway to your car, right?"

"Believe me, I'm seriously thinking about it."

Cassie sighed. This one full of her usual scorn. "Stop running away, Nick. You never used to be a runner, but now that's all you do anymore. I thought I saw some of the old spark in you when that C.I. of yours was murdered last year. I thought I saw a man who cared again. But now it seems you've gone right back into whatever hole you keep burying yourself in."

"I repeat. Fuck you."

"Dammit, Nick. The girl's husband is missing, okay? The department has done what it can, but you know what it's like. We have other cases that take priority. If I knew anyone else who could help her, believe me, I wouldn't have bothered you. But you were the best once, and you have access to a world that I can only begin to penetrate. The moment I try, the rats smell blue and start scattering."

"What are you talking about? Who is she involved with?"

"Just listen to her story and you'll understand."

Then the line once again went dead and she was gone.

"We came here on our honeymoon," Rachel said. "Almost two months ago to the day."

The absence of the band had made the Big 8 Lounge considerably more tolerable. The room lights had been brought up slightly, and Jennings could actually see without the aid of pyrotechnics.

He sat in the booth again, nursing a glass of scotch as he waited for Rachel to tell her story. Even before Cassie hung up on him he'd known that he would talk to the girl. But it was a struggle. He couldn't stop staring at her, couldn't stop seeing his baby all grown up, as beautiful as a life fulfilled.

She sat across from him, her blue eyes focused on her hands. She seemed to have lost herself for a moment, and Jennings prompted her. "So that was in May."

She looked up at him and nodded. "We booked a room at the Palace, a deluxe suite with all the bells and whistles. Trevor wouldn't tell me how much it all cost, but I'm sure it was a lot."

"Could he afford it?"

"I thought so at the time. His parents were killed by a drunk driver when we were still in college and he inherited quite a bit of money from them. His dad was a personal injury attorney who got a big payoff for some lawsuit against a hospital. He turned around and invested in stocks and real estate and wound up making more money than any single person should have a right to." She paused. "There's something unseemly about that kind of wealth, don't you think? With all the people who are starving. I promised Trevor I'd never tell him what to do with his money, but that I hoped he realized how fortunate we are."

"And did he?"

She nodded. "He's never been the type to flaunt what he has. Except for the honeymoon. He wanted to make it special, because *we* were special. That's what he said. That the two of us together are like parts of a song. We each have our own melody, but when we're blended together, that's when the magic happens."

Jennings thought about the band that had vacated the stage and wasn't so sure this was always true. But he appreciated the sentiment, even if it was a little sugary.

"So what happened the night he went missing?"

Rachel sucked in a breath and was silent for a moment, once again turning inward.

"We fought," she said. "Can you believe that? We fought on our honeymoon."

Jennings shrugged. "It happens sometimes."

She shook her head. "Not like this. I was so angry I could have killed him, because if the previous three days had shown me anything, it was that I hadn't married the man I thought I had."

"How was he different?"

"It was like I'd somehow run away with his evil twin," she said. "Oh, the first day was fine. We spent some time in the casino, then went up to the room and did what you're supposed to do on your honeymoon. But around four o'clock that morning, I woke up and Trevor wasn't in bed. So I got dressed and went looking for him and found him downstairs in one of the poker rooms playing Texas Hold 'em. He looked exhausted and wired and I suspected he'd been there for hours. Probably left the room the minute I fell asleep."

"And this surprised you?"

"I never thought of him as much of a gambler. Oh, he'd sometimes play poker with his roommates in college, but it was never a big deal. When I saw him that morning, there was something about the look on his face that scared me. He didn't have many chips left and there was a kind of desperation in his eyes that reminded me of a friend of mine who got hooked on diet pills. If she didn't get her dose, she turned into an absolute head case. She was impossible to be around unless she was drugged."

Jennings fully understood that kind of desperation. He'd felt a bit of it only an hour earlier as he'd stared at those two lonely deuces and knew his time at the table was likely to be short.

"So what do you think the problem was?" he asked.

"At the time, I didn't know. And believe me, I was worried. I mean, here's a guy who barely gambles, looking like he's been chipping heroin for at least a decade. It was like I'd gone to bed with Dr. Jekyll and woke up to Mr. Hyde. He was loud and nasty to me, and the dealer finally asked us to take it outside, because our little domestic drama was disturbing the other players. So I left crying and went up to the room but Trevor didn't come back for another three hours. And the minute he walked through the door, I could see that he was back to his old self."

"Because he'd been winning again."

"Right," she said. "How did you know?"

"You're story isn't particularly unique."

Jennings own addiction had never manifested into such dramatic mood swings, but he recognized the behavior. Trevor Brennan was a hard core gambler and it hadn't happened over the course of one night. He wasn't Jekyll and Hyde, but all Hyde, using his wits and acting skills to keep those around him from seeing who he really was.

Chances were good you'd find hundreds of old lottery tickets in his desk drawer, or the names and numbers of bookies around his hometown. He'd watch the local and national basketball scores with a little more intensity than your average fan, and if his team lost he'd take it harder than their head coach. Those college poker games may have been the start of it all, or could merely have been a symptom of a fully developed compulsion.

"Who made the decision to come to Vegas for your honeymoon?"

"Trevor did."

"And did that seem unusual to you?"

"I didn't really think about it. I'd never been here before, but Trevor had, and said we'd have a blast. And since we didn't want to have a big wedding or anything—my parents are gone, too—we figured we'd come here and get married and celebrate until our legs were shaking." She flushed suddenly and looked away from him. "Sorry, I guess that was a bit TMI."

Jennings waved the notion aside. "Let's get back to the night he went missing."

She took a moment, once again finding comfort in her fidgeting fingers. "So anyway, it went like that for two more days, and each day the good Trevor seemed to fade away as the bad Trevor took over. That last night, when he told me he was going out for while, I finally couldn't take it anymore and started shouting at him. Told him if he didn't pull himself together, I'd divorce him or have the marriage annulled. It was the worst fight we'd ever had, and in the middle of it all, he finally broke down and confessed what was going on."

"Let me guess," Jennings said. "He was broke."

She looked surprised. "How did you know?"

"Because that's how it always goes."

"He told me he'd frittered away most of his parents' money on bad investments and gambling debts. He'd fired all his financial people and was about to lose both his houses and wasn't even sure he had enough to pay for our hotel bill. I couldn't even fathom how somebody with all that money could wind up like that, and it was a shock to the system, to say the least. He kept promising that if I just gave him a little more time, had a little more faith, he'd build it all back up again."

"And how did he plan to do that?"

"He said he'd met some Russian or Ukrainian guy in the casino who offered to cut him in on a game they had going. Not a scam, exactly, but there were a couple of ringers at the table—real players like Trevor—pitted against a bunch of obscenely rich amateurs who had no idea it was more than just a friendly game. He promised Trevor he'd quadruple his stake, guaranteed."

Which meant at least one of the other "real" players was a card mechanic, and this not-exactly-a-scam was exactly that, the target being none other than Trevor Brennan himself, who had proven he knew how to lose.

Gambling in Vegas was tightly controlled, but there was an entire poker underground that operated just below the radar, always looking for big fish—or "whales"—with fat wallets and meager playing skills. Some of those who targeted them utilized cheats, while others simply relied on superior playing skill to outwit their marks.

Jennings now understood the true reason Cassie had sent Rachel to him for help. The appeal to sentiment was real, but far less important than the expertise he could offer. Jennings frequently traveled among these people and had a number of friends who wouldn't look at him sideways if he started asking questions.

"So I assume you let him go?" Jennings asked.

"I didn't *let* him do anything. I couldn't have stopped him if I tried. So I stood there crying and watched him walk out the door.

He didn't even kiss me before he left."

"And that was the last time you saw him?"

Tears sprang to her eyes as she nodded. She quickly wiped at them with the back of her hand, and he could see that despite her apparent strength, this had nearly broken her. The fact that she had stayed in Vegas and even found a job here, was a fairly good indication that she wasn't about to let him go.

Jennings had no idea what she wanted from him. The guy was gone and it was likely that he was never coming back. If he was as broke and desperate as he had claimed, then it was also likely he'd found himself in deep trouble with some very nasty people, the outcome of which was rarely good.

At this point, two months on, Trevor Brennan was bound to be nothing more than a scattered pile of bones in the desert, baked by the sun and gnawed on by coyotes. Whether he was the victim of thugs or took his own life was a question that would probably never be answered.

"You do realize," Jennings told her, "that he's more than likely dead."

She shook her head. "Cassie said you would help me. That's not helping. And it's not true."

"I'm just trying to be realistic, Ms. Brennan. Vegas may bill itself as the world's biggest playground, but it can be a very dicey place for anyone who doesn't understand the rules. This isn't like that movie where Trevor's stuck up on a hotel roof getting a sunburn. If your husband got himself involved with the kind of people I think he did, and if he pissed them off in any way—"

She slapped a hand on the table. "You're not listening to me. He isn't dead, I *know* he isn't."

Her vehemence startled some nearby patrons. They turned to look, but Jennings stared them down, then returned his attention to Rachel Brennan.

"I suppose there's always that chance," he said, telling her what she wanted to hear. "But it isn't likely."

She shook her head emphatically. "No, Mr. Jennings. You don't understand. I know for *sure* he isn't dead. There's no question about it."

"And how do you know this?"

"Because he called me last night."

5

She had just finished her shift, she told Jennings, and was walking to her car when her phone rang. She always carried it with her—the same phone she'd brought on their honeymoon—because she didn't want to chance missing any attempts at contact. She'd even purchased a new phone for every day use, reserving the older one exclusively for Trevor.

"When I heard the ring, I couldn't quite believe it at first. Thought I must be hallucinating. I mean, I'd been waiting for weeks to hear it and all of a sudden there it was."

She had reached into her bag with shaky hands and when she saw that the screen said UNKNOWN CALLER, she thought it might be a misdial or a telemarketer looking to make her life miserable. She clicked it on, answered with a tentative "...Trevor?" and was both surprised and relieved when she heard his voice.

"...Baby?"

"Oh my God. Oh my God. Trevor, where are you? What happened to you?"

The connection was bad, his voice shredded by digital interference. "Oh, Rachel... ank God. ...on't know... long I can stay on the... but—"

"Slow down," she said. "You're breaking up. I can barely understand—"

"...help me, babe. ...ou have to... me. You wouldn't believe... I've... going through."

His voice sounded weak and strained.

"Tell me what to do," she said. "Tell me where to find you."

"...elp me..." he repeated. "You have to—"

A digital squawk cut him off, followed by dead silence. She waited for something more, but nothing came. Just an empty void.

"Trevor?"

She waited and got nothing.

"Trevor?"

Still nothing.

"*TREVOR?*"

But he was gone. And he hadn't called her back.

She had tried calling *him* back, but the line just rang and rang. And rang.

Jennings thought the story sounded melodramatic and unrealistic, like something pulled from an episode of must-see TV. But as he watched her tell it, he saw a sincerity in her eyes that was hard to fake. It was certainly possible that she was playing some kind of angle, but to what end? Simply to convince him to help her? That didn't seem likely, although it was a possibility he had to consider.

"Did you talk to the police about this call?"

"Of course I did. The minute I realized Trevor wasn't on the line, I called Cassie and told her what had happened. She was the one assigned to the case when he first disappeared."

"And what did she say?"

"She asked me to come in this morning and we went straight to her captain hoping he'd let her follow up. She'd told me that because the case was cold, he was hesitant to devote too many resources to it, but she was sure Trevor's phone call would change his mind."

"Obviously it didn't."

She shook her head. "He thought I'd made it all up to get them interested in the case again. He's convinced this is nothing more than Trevor getting cold feet a couple days too late. When he wouldn't authorize her to pursue it, Cassie suggested I come talk to you. And here we are."

"So did you?"

She looked confused. "Did I what?"

"Make it all up."

She did a slow burn, her cheeks going red, and in that moment Jennings saw his daughter even more than before. Her expression was nearly identical to one Michelle would adopt when her integrity was challenged. A slow burn followed by indignant anger.

"Do you think this is a game to me?"

"No, I think you're quite serious. But you're also desperate to find the man you love, and desperate people sometimes do foolish things. And a false lead is worse than no leads at all, because it might send us off in the wrong direc—"

"I'm telling you, he called me. I didn't make it up, okay?"

"Okay, okay, but I had to ask. And if Cassie thinks there's something there, that's good enough for me."

Her anger subsided and she looked hopeful. "So you'll help me?"

"I'm not sure there's a whole lot I can do at this point. I'm glad you heard from him. That makes this all a bit less bleak than I originally thought, but the call didn't exactly give us much to go on. Are you sure you gave the conversation to me verbatim?"

"Yes."

"He didn't say what *kind* of trouble he might be in, or how you might contact him?"

"No, I told you everything. The connection was bad and he was hard to understand. All I can hope for is that he calls me again."

Jennings nodded, but there was a possible scenario forming in his mind. "Do you have any money yourself, Ms. Brennan?"

"I can pay you, if that's what you're worried about."

"No," he said, waving her off. "I don't care about that."

He knew he *should* care, because he was dead broke, but he couldn't look at that face and take money from her.

"When I see you wearing a Keno uniform and working in a dump like the Four Jacks," he continued, "I make the logical assumption that you took the job in order to survive while you're here in Vegas. Is that true?"

"What difference does it make?"

"Maybe a big one."

She sighed. "The answer is no. I don't really need the money. But I've been working jobs on and off ever since I was fifteen, and it doesn't make any sense to me to sit around by some hotel pool and fret day after day as I wait for something to happen. That would just drive me crazy. And this was the first job that came along. I'm good at it and it occupies my mind."

Rachel Brennan wasn't the only person of means that Jennings had seen go that route. Some people, no matter how much money they had, felt a need to keep moving, keep the blood circulating and the mind working. And if they lacked the entrepreneurial spirit, they simply took work that they found interesting and fulfilling.

During his career on the force, Jennings had known two detectives, both born into rich families, who never had to work a day in their lives. One of them, a SWAT team member dubbed Richie Rich by his squad mates, had personally donated enough funds to buy the unit an armored tank.

But taking a job as a cop was a far cry from running Keno cards, and Jennings could only shake his head at the thought.

"So then how much are you worth?" he asked.

"Does that really matter?"

"It may."

She shrugged. "I don't know for sure. I leave all that stuff to my financial people. But let's just say I could probably go the rest of my life without working—which would be pretty sad, if you ask me."

Jennings nodded. "And I assume Trevor knew this?"

"Of course he did. That was one of the things that brought us together during senior year. We had both lost our parents around the same time and had inherited quite a bit of money. We met at one of the grief counseling sessions the school makes available for students."

"So when he went broke, he didn't ask you for any money?"

"No. He wouldn't do that. It was a matter of pride with him. We've always kept our finances separate." She paused. "Why is all that so important to you?"

"I'm trying to weigh the situation and look at it from as many different angles as I can."

"I don't understand."

Jennings thought she might, but was choosing not to let her mind go in that direction. He, on the other hand, was an ex-cop who had seen just about all there was to see, and the vagueness of that phone call from Trevor had raised his natural suspicions. Had this girl gotten herself caught up in a very long con? Was it possible that everything that had happened since she and Trevor met was designed to separate her from some or all of her inheritance?

It seemed far-fetched—as far-fetched as the phone call itself—and it made no sense to launch a confidence game that might get the police involved, but you never knew. Maybe Trevor Brennan was playing Rachel for a sucker.

But even if he wasn't, even if he'd been Mr. Tried and True, there was still a possibility that somebody was taking advantage of her vulnerability.

"One last question," Jennings said. "And I don't want you to get angry. It's just a question."

She looked guarded. "Okay. What?"

"This voice on the phone. Are you absolutely sure it was your husband?"

"What do you mean, am I sure?"

"You said yourself that the connection was bad. Is it possible that someone else could have been pretending to—"

"No," she said. "I *know* it was Trevor. I know his voice."

"Then I guess the first thing we need to do is find out where that call originated from."

"That's what Cassandra said. I gave her permission to request my cell phone records and she promised to look into it, even though her boss told her to leave it alone. I really don't like that man."

"I used to work with the guy and, trust me, nobody does."

"So will you help me?"

She looked at him with another of his daughter's patented expressions—a mix of hope and anticipation—and as hard as he tried, Jennings couldn't convince himself to walk away. He wasn't sure there was a lot he could do, but he had to try. If not for Rachel Brennan, then in memory of Michelle, who had never gotten her own justice.

"Just tell me this," he said. "Do you still love him? Or are you doing this out of some sense of marital obligation?"

"Of course I love him. I wouldn't be asking you if I didn't."

He nodded. "All right, then. I'll do my best. And lately that's a lot more than most people get out of me."

She reached across the table and squeezed his hand. "Thank you, Mr. Jennings."

"Nick," he said. "Call me Nick."

"Your boss is an idiot."

Jennings was sitting in his Vic in the lot behind the Four Jacks, and had known that Cassie would pick up when he called again. Like him, she was a night owl and never went to bed before one a.m.

Besides, she had a vested interest in this case.

"My boss is many things," she told him. "Most of which I can't say out loud."

"Captain Goddamn Bean Counter. Right now I'd get great satisfaction in kicking his Brooks Brothers ass."

"You'd have to stand in a very long line," she said, then paused. "I take it this is about Rachel?"

"She tells me you're looking into her phone records. Just wondering what you found."

"Does this mean you're in?"

"Don't start gloating. It isn't attractive. But yeah, I'm in. Although I don't know how much use I'll be. About all I can do is shake a few trees and see what falls out."

"That's all I ask."

"So did you get anything on that call or not?"

"I couldn't do it officially, so let me check my email, see if my friend at the phone company came through."

She put him on hold and he took the time to think about the late nights they used to spend at home together, back when the world was a far more tolerable place. Jennings watching the tube while Cassie curled her legs under her in the armchair next to him and read a book. They could go a whole night with little more than a sentence between them, but that didn't matter. Not for a second. There was a comfort and safety and love there that made words both unnecessary and irrelevant.

Now the words always seemed to get in the way.

She finally came back on the line. "We're in luck—my friend came through. Seems the call from Trevor Brennan originated from a pay phone at the Bar Vista Poker Club."

Jennings was surprised. "They still make pay phones?"

"It was probably installed when the place was built sixty years ago."

"Good point. So that's it? That's all we've got?"

"That and the Palace," she said. "Where the husband was originally approached to play an off the grid game. But when we first opened the investigation, we showed his picture around to all the employees on duty that day and nobody even remembered seeing him."

"Were any of them Russian? Or Ukrainian?"

"No, why do ask?"

"Because Rachel said her husband told her he was approached by one or the other."

"That's weird. She never mentioned that detail."

"Maybe it just came to her as she was rehashing the story for me. Anyway, I'm guessing the guy was a scout, keeping an eye out for gullible whales."

"We went that way, too, but were never able to turn up anything."

"I assume you ran a background check on the husband?"

"Yeah, he checked out. No priors, nothing. He seems to be exactly what she said he was."

"What about his financials? Was that inheritance story real?"

"We couldn't confirm that, but he *did* have money at one point, most of which is gone."

Jennings sighed. "I can't believe I'm letting myself get involved in this."

"I never doubted it for a minute."

Getting hold of Scully by phone was never easy. The guy traded burners every other day and Jennings never knew if the number he had was a working one. The straightest path to contact was to head on over to the Pin Drop Lounge to see if he was parked at a table there.

Nine times out of ten he was.

At a quarter to one, Jennings pushed through the doors of the Golden Sands Bowling Alley and looked out at the sea of late-night bowlers crowding the lanes. The familiar rumble and muted clatter of ball against pins was almost soothing to his ears, reminding him of the many nights he'd spent here playing for the

LVMPD League, and the many nights since, planning money-making strategies with Scully.

In a way, this place felt more like home than his crummy one-bedroom walk up.

True to form, Scully sat at his usual table in the lounge. If they had business to discuss, Jennings would give him a wave and they'd go out to the lanes or the snack bar, where the sounds of the bowlers would keep them safe from prying ears.

Tonight was different, so Jennings went over to the table and sat.

"You've got an in with someone over at the Bar Vista Poker Club right?"

Scully looked up from his racing form. "What—not even a hello?"

"Just answer the question."

"I've got an in with a lot of someones at a lot of different places."

Jennings sighed. "Now is not the time to be coy, my friend. Do you or don't you?"

"As a matter of fact I do. A tasty little redhead named Anita Kool —with a K—who wanted to be a showgirl but wound up serving watered down drinks to sleeze buckets with a jones for poker. "

"Anita *Kool*?"

Scully shrugged. "She swears it's her real name. But then she also swears her tits are real. Why are you asking? You know a few people over there yourself, don't you?"

Jennings shook his head. "Just Billy Ives, but he's been dead for a couple years."

"Ahh, good old Billy. I've never understood what compels a man to shoot himself in the head like that."

"Let's get back to Anita, okay? You think you could make an introduction?"

"That depends," Scully said. "What's this about?"

Jennings saw no harm in telling him and gave him the full rundown.

Scully shook his head. "So this is what? Some kind of knight in shining armor thing? Like with that ex-hooker you got yourself involved with last year? Don't forget how that turned out."

"I'm not forgetting anything. I did what needed to be done."

"You want my advice, Nick, stay the hell out of it. If this guy's hanging out at the BVP club, he isn't somebody you—and especially his blushing bride—should be associating yourselves with. Who's to say this isn't some elaborate scheme to bilk her out of her fortune?"

"Believe me, I went there, too, but two months later? That doesn't make much sense."

"Are you kidding me? Two months is nothing. I knew a guy who ran a con for two and a half years. At two months she's primed to be just desperate enough to pay anything to get her long lost hubby back."

"Maybe. But I'm not feeling it. Are you gonna make the introduction or not?"

Scully sighed and pulled out one of his burners. "All right, I'll give Anita a call, but consider yourself warned. You may be stepping into something very nasty."

"Wouldn't be the first time," Jennings said.

7

The Bar Vista Poker Club was located on South Las Vegas Boulevard, a small, squat building nestled between an Econo gas station and a dingy looking tattoo parlor.

It was nearly two a.m. when Jennings stepped inside, but the six tables that crowded the room were all crowded themselves, career winners and losers of all shapes and sizes drawing and ditching cards and fingering chips.

Jennings instinctively looked for an empty chair, but had to remind himself that he wasn't here for play, and didn't have the cash to get into a game anyway. But he felt the itch coming on, that need to be part of the action, and knew he had to watch himself or he'd pull out his only working credit card and ask for an advance.

Looking to his left, toward the bar, he saw an attractive redhead in a short skirt and halter top picking up drinks from the bartender.

He went over to her. "Anita Kool?"

She gave him a quick look, then went back to her task, placing a couple of draft beers onto a small round tray. He guessed that she was about forty-two or so, but still slim and toned, with breasts that were disproportionately large and clearly not natural. But they looked good on her. And it didn't hurt that she was quite beautiful.

"Let me guess," she said. "You're Scully's friend."

He held out a hand. "Nick Jennings."

She studied him more slowly as she shook it and seemed to like what she saw. "You used to be a cop, right?"

"Guilty as charged."

"One of my ex-boyfriends was a cop. Real nasty bastard. But he was always great in bed. Are you great in bed, Nick?"

"I'm not really into self-analysis."

She smiled. "Most men aren't. But I'm thinking you probably get good marks, though I guess you aren't here to be graded. Scully was pretty cryptic on the phone. So what is it you need from little old me?"

"Just a couple minutes of your time. Ask you a few questions."

Her smile faded. "What kind of questions?"

"About a friend of mine who's missing. Maybe you can help me find him."

"I don't see how, but let me drop off this order and I'll be right with you." She pointed. "There's an empty booth in back."

Jennings thanked her and went to the booth as she hoisted the tray above her shoulder and sashayed her way through the tables, smiling and chatting with several of the players as she moved. The rear view was as pleasant as the front, and it was obvious she was well liked around here, and only partly because of her sizable chest.

Jennings sat and waited until she delivered her drinks and came over to him.

"Okay," she said, sliding in across the table. "Who's this friend of yours?"

"A guy by the name of Trevor Brennan. I don't suppose that name rings a bell? "

"Should it?"

Jennings shook his head. "No reason. But it was worth a shot." He reached into his coat pocket, pulled out a small snapshot that Rachel had given him, then placed it on the table and slid it across to her. The photo was taken at the Little White Wedding Chapel not that far down the street. "This is him."

Anita looked down at it, studying it carefully. Trevor was a big, muscular man who obviously took care of himself. Judging by his expression, he didn't lack confidence, either.

"He was in here last night at approximately eleven p.m.," Jennings told her. "He made a call from that pay phone." He pointed to a hallway that led to the restrooms, where a sixties era pay phone was mounted on the wall near the men's room. "In the age of cell phones, that's a little unusual, isn't it?"

She snorted. "You'd be surprised how many people use that piece of junk. Especially after they've hocked their cell for some cash. Dimitri's got a whole collection he sells on Ebay."

Jennings perked up. "Dimitri?"

Could this be Trevor's Russian?

"He's what qualifies as a manager around here."

Jennings nodded and gestured to the pay phone. "The person

my friend called tried calling him back after they got cut off. Said the line just rang and rang."

Anita shrugged. "That's no big surprise. Thing rings all the time, but usually nobody answers it unless they're expecting a call or they're suffering from OCD." She looked back at the photo again. "I'm sorry, but this guy doesn't look familiar. We get a lot of players coming and going, and after awhile most of them tend to blend together."

"You're sure you don't remember him?"

"I'm sure," she said.

"What about the bartender? Was he working last night?"

She shook her head. "Dicky Mars was on last night. He'll be back tomorrow."

Jennings sighed and reached into his jacket pocket, taking out one of his old LVMPD calling cards. He didn't know why he'd kept them, but they sometimes came in handy. He had scratched out his old office number and penciled in his cell.

"Do me a favor," he said, handing her the card. "Have Dicky give me a call at this number. Can you do that for me?"

She smiled and the card quickly disappeared into her cleavage. "I could do a lot for you, hon, if you don't mind overly aggressive females. You look like you could use a..." She stiffened, looking past his shoulder. "Oh, shit."

"What's wrong?"

"I didn't think he'd be in tonight."

"Who?" Jennings asked and turned to look.

A massive wall of cement with arms and legs and profoundly Slavic features came in through the front door, his gaze taking in the room. Within seconds he zeroed in on Jennings and Anita and headed in their direction, a hostile expression taking form.

Or maybe that was how he always looked.

"That's Dimitri," she said quietly. "My boss."

Dimitri came over to the table and grabbed Anita by the upper arm, yanking her roughly out of the booth. "Who say you sit down? You work."

Anita winced and Jennings jumped to his feet. "Whoa there, big guy. Let the lady go."

Dimitri swiveled his head. "Who are you, tell me my business?"

"Police," Jennings said. "Now let her go."

Dimitri gave him the once over as if he wasn't quite sure Jennings was telling the truth, but finally let her go. "She not sit down. She have work to do."

"It was just for a second," Anita said, rubbing her arm. And it was clear that she was afraid of this guy. Very much so. "He was asking me about a friend of his, is all."

Dimitri frowned. "What friend?"

She gestured to the photo on the table. "He was in here last night and used the pay phone."

Dimitri looked at the photo and for an instant Jennings thought he saw a subtle shift in the man's eyes.

Surprise? Recognition?

Or had he imagined it?

"He nobody," Dimitri barked. "Pay phone broken. Been broken for over year." He looked at Jennings. "Take your photo and go away, police man. Don't bother my worker."

"He wasn't bothering me, Dimi—"

"You shut up, or you go, too. Is that what you want?"

She looked stricken. "No," she said. "I need this job."

"Then do what I pay for."

She shot Jennings a glance and hurried back to the bar, where another round of drinks was waiting for her.

Dimitri scowled at her, then scooped up the photo of Trevor Brennan from the table and shoved it toward Jennings. "You don't hear me? Leave."

Jennings took it from him. "You know, my mother always said you can catch more flies with honey than vinegar."

"Why I need flies? I don't need catch flies."

"Never mind." Jennings held the photograph out. "You sure you don't want to take another look? I know that pay phone still works, so I'm wondering why you would lie about something like that?"

"I don't like politsiya in my club. They make bad business."

"If you've seen this guy, you need to tell me, Dimitri. Because I'd be happy to invite all my cop friends to join me here for a game of stud."

Dimitri took a step toward Jennings. "Maybe I do catch fly.

Maybe I pinch wings."

They stood there, facing each other, Jennings's eye line slightly south of the guy's massive shoulders. If they traded blows, Jennings knew he was likely to wind up in the hospital or worse, but he'd be damned if he'd let this son of a bitch intimidate him.

"You'd better turn that frown upside down, my friend, or you'll regret it."

"You threaten me?"

Jennings held up the photo one more time. "I just want an answer to my question. You sure you maybe didn't see this guy at the Palace a couple months ago and invite him to a private game?"

Dimitri surprised him with a smile that looked like something out of an old Hammer horror film. He took the photo, but instead of looking at it, slowly tore it in half and let the pieces flutter to the floor.

"Fuck your friend and fuck you, too," he said, then stomped off toward a hallway and pushed his way through a door marked OFFICE.

There wasn't much Jennings could add to that.

Crouching down, he scooped up the pieces of the photograph, then gave Anita Kool a sympathetic nod and headed back out into the Vegas heat.

8

He was halfway up the steps to his apartment when his phone rang.

It was getting a real workout tonight.

He checked the screen, saw the UNKNOWN CALLER tag and debated letting voicemail pick up. But then his curiosity got the better of him and he answered. "Nick Jennings."

"You really have a bedroom voice, you know that? Goes with the bedroom eyes."

Jennings frowned and continued up the steps. "Who is this?"

"You've forgotten so soon? I'm insulted. I've been keeping that card you gave me nice and warm."

"Ms. Kool?"

"Anita. And I'm sorry to bother you at such a godless hour, but I figured you'd still be awake. I'm guessing you've got a wee bit of vampire blood in you, and I do like my vampires."

"I thought zombies were the thing these days."

"Been there, done that, and no thanks. My ex was a zombie times ten. That's why he's my ex."

Jennings reached the top of the steps and started down the concrete hallway toward his door. "I assume you have a reason for calling me?"

"Oh, don't be like that. But yes, I thought you might want to know that the minute you left the club, the extension on the house phone behind the bar started lighting up like crazy. Dimitri in his office making calls—which, believe me, is not his style. He's more of a grunter than a communicator."

"I kinda got that vibe."

"Anyway, when Buddy the bartender was in back getting more ice, I took a little listen to see if I could figure out what it was all about."

"And?"

"He was speaking Russian, so I didn't understand much, but I did hear the word politsiya a few times, so I'm guessing they were talking about you."

"Who's they?" Jennings asked.

"I'm pretty sure the guy on the line with him was either Alexey or his brother. It's hard to tell them apart."

Jennings stiffened. He knew the name, but had to be sure. "Alexey?"

"Alexey Kozlov. The man who owns the club and about ten others around town. A real sweetheart who makes Dimitri seem like a charm school graduate."

"I've heard of him," Jennings said.

Alexey Kozlov was a former KGB agent who had immigrated to Nevada after the end of the cold war and had his fingers in a dozen different criminal enterprises, including sex trafficking and a very lucrative drug trade. Prostitution was legal in Nevada, but not in Vegas proper, and Kozlov made sure that businessmen and lonely husbands didn't have to travel outside the city limits for companionship. He had been on the LVMPD's radar for several years, but had never been exposed enough to be collared.

"Anyway," Anita said, "I figured you'd want to know. Although I would much rather have delivered the news in person."

Jennings smiled. "I'm afraid your expectations are a bit high."

"I thought you didn't do self-analysis."

"I'm a liar," he said.

"Most men are. But as long as you're still awake, maybe you'd be interested in a therapy session. I'm practically certificated and everything."

"You don't give up, do you?"

"Do you really want me to?"

Jennings thought about this. He hadn't been with a woman in quite some time, and it might be just the thing to quell the itch that had been crawling through his intestines, working its way up toward his chest. Maybe Anita Kool, with her impossible name and aggressive manner, was just what he needed to keep it from reaching his brain. Because once that happened he'd be in serious trouble. And he couldn't afford to be in serious trouble.

"No," he said. "I guess I don't."

"Well, now, that's what I like to hear. Give me your address and I'll catch a cab right over."

He reeled it off, then quickly went inside to take a shower.

"You smell clean," she said.

"I'm not a complete heathen. I do bathe once in awhile."

They were sitting on his couch, which, before she arrived had been piled with newspapers and a couple boxes of casino decks that Jennings used in his card act. He had stuffed everything into his hall closet and quickly run the vacuum, finishing up only moments before his doorbell rang.

Now, despite the hour, they had glasses of wine in hand and the low hum of smooth jazz on the stereo. Jennings wasn't accustomed to entertaining, but he made do with what he had.

"You're not a heathen at all," she said. "You even cleaned up for me."

"How did you know?"

"I heard the vacuum running and waited until you were done before I rang the bell. You've just met me and already you're trying to impress. I like that."

"To be honest, I'm a little out of practice for this kind of thing."

She smiled. "It's just like riding a bicycle."

He grinned and shook his head. "No, I mean having people over to my place. It's been a long time and I've logged a lot of miles since then."

"Is that why you seem so sad?"

She'd surprised him. "What do you mean?"

"It's just a feeling I got the moment I saw you. You come on tough, like the way you did with Dimitri, but you have that lost lamb look that makes a girl want to cuddle with you and tell you it'll be okay." She reached out and ran a hand over his shoulder. "Are you a lost lamb, Nick?"

"I don't know about lost, but I've seen better times."

"Uh-huh. Who is she?"

"She?"

"The woman you're pining for. The one you wish were here instead of me."

"Boy, you really cut to the heart of the matter, don't you."

"I've been blunt since the day I was born and I've never seen a reason to change. I'm not interested in being anyone's good time girl, but I don't mind playing surrogate now and again. And you look like you really could use that therapy we talked about." She paused. "But you didn't answer my question. Who is she?"

"It's a long, boring story."

"No longer or more boring than mine, I'm sure. So tell me. I'm listening."

Jennings studied her, wondering why he felt compelled to open up to this woman. He barely knew her, for Christ's sake, yet there was something about her frankness that appealed to him.

"Come on," she said. "I won't bite."

It took him a moment. Then he said, "When I was a cop my wife Cassie and I were the toast of the department. I worked Homicide and she worked in the Special Victims Unit. Life was good—great, in fact, but then something terrible happened to us—something I'd rather not get into, but would never wish on another human being. And while she managed to move past it, to get on with her life and career, I pretty much hit rock bottom and in the process almost got my partner killed. After that, I was a pariah in the department and Cassie said she didn't know me anymore. And she didn't. I didn't even know myself."

"So she divorced you."

Jennings nodded. "And I've never blamed her. I felt relieved when she did. Because I was a burden to her and I didn't want to be that burden. I wanted to be what I was before. But I knew there was no way I'd ever get back there." He paused, thinking about that terrible time and wishing he could bleach it all from his brain. "Shortly before the divorce I was unceremoniously kicked off the force and here I am today, four years later, still scrambling, still wondering if I'll ever dig my way out of this hole."

"Have you ever asked for help?"

"I'm not the asking type."

"So you lock yourself up in this apartment and try to cope alone? That's not healthy."

"I'm not exactly a hermit," he said. "I get out and do things, hang with Scully. And despite his flaws, he's turned out to be a very good friend."

"Scully's flaws are what make him so lovable."

Jennings smiled. "He's one of a kind."

She nodded vaguely and they were silent for a moment. Then she set her wine glass on the coffee table. "I don't know, Nick. You seem like damaged goods to me. So I guess it's a good thing I specialize in repairing damage."

"You do, do you?"

"I've got my own tragic story, so I know a kindred spirit when I see one. But we'll get into that some other time, if you're still interested in hanging around with me after tonight."

She leaned forward and kissed him, tenderly at first, then a little more assertively, drawing his tongue into her mouth.

She smelled and tasted like no other woman he had ever kissed.

He pulled away. "I'm thinking I may be very interested."

"Good, because I'm starting to like you."

"You didn't before?"

"Wanting and liking are two different things. It's kind of nice when they go together."

Her hands fell to his belt buckle and she unfastened it, then slipped off the couch and got on her knees, pulling his pants down and off. A moment later she was kneeling between his legs, her hands stroking him through his boxers.

Jennings's phone went off again, braying in his coat that hung over the dining room chair. He groaned and listened for a moment, wondering if he should answer. But then he decided no, that this was *his* time now and he didn't want it interrupted.

Anita didn't flinch once as it rang. Kept doing what she was doing and it felt very good indeed.

"This is step number one of your therapy session, Nick. By the time we get to step five, both of us will have completely forgotten our troubles..."

"That would be a pretty neat trick," he said.

"I know a lot of neat tricks."

9

When his phone rang again later that morning, Jennings wanted to stomp it flat. It seemed he'd had more calls in the last twenty-four hours than he'd received the entire year, and he vowed right then and there to change his number.

He was in bed, only half awake, the morning sun streaming in through his window, the phone chiming faintly in the living room where he'd left it. Anita Kool's smooth rear end was pressed up against him as she slept, and he remembered being inside her and felt himself stirring, wanting to be there again.

Instead, he forced himself to get up, then dragged his ass into the living room. He found his phone in his coat pocket, pulled it out and saw the name on the screen.

Cassie again.

He immediately felt guilty. They hadn't lived together in years, hadn't been intimate in any way, but in his mind he had cheated on her with Anita and the thought didn't sit well in his gut.

It was an irrational feeling, but a potent one.

Flicking his thumb across the screen, he finally answered, catching it just before it went to voicemail. "Hey, Cass, what's up?"

The receiver exploded with the sound of her voice. "Why do you take so goddamn long to answer your phone?"

"That's a nice hello."

"I'm not interested in nice right now. What the hell happened last night?"

Jennings frowned, wondering what she was so upset about. "What do you mean? I told you what happened."

"After we spoke, did you go back and see Rachel again?"

"No. I went over to the BVP club to check out Trevor's phone call. I think I may have stirred up the nest a bit, but I didn't have any luck. At least not the kind I was hoping for."

That twinge of guilt tugged at him.

"And you didn't take Rachel with you?"

"No," he said. "Why would I do that? Contrary to popular belief, I'm not stupid. It's bad enough she works at the Jacks. She doesn't need to be hanging around places like the BVP. Now what the hell is going on?"

"I'm at county right now. Rachel was attacked last night."

"*What?*"

He heard a hitch in Cassie's voice. "It's bad, Nick. The doctors had to induce a coma. They're not sure she's going to make it."

"You've gotta be fucking kidding me."

"I wish I were," she said. "I wish I were."

He was pulling on his clothes when he remembered the call he hadn't answered last night. It had come around three-thirty or so, as Anita Kool was making her move on the sofa.

Dread growing in his gut, he headed back out to the living room and snatched the phone up off the coffee table. When he checked the notifications bar, lo and behold, a little blue flag told him he had voicemail.

Shit.

He immediately tapped the screen and brought up the recording, listening intently as Rachel Brennan's anxious voice filled his ear, his heart sinking with every word.

"Mr. Jennings—Nick—I know it's late, but if you get this message, please call me back as soon as possible. I heard from Trevor again and he wants me to meet him and I don't really want to go alone. I'll wait for your call as long as I can, but if I don't go soon, I'm afraid I'll never hear from him again."

Jennings continued listening as Rachel went away and a robotic voice asked him if he wanted to save or delete the message.

He clicked off, left a note for Anita, and grabbed his keys.

10

"She has multiple fractures and a brain hemorrhage," Cassie said. "They induced the coma shortly after they brought her in, in hopes of giving her brain a rest to reduce the swelling. But they don't sound optimistic."

Jennings stood with her near the nurse's station of the Intensive Care Unit at Clark County General. Through a windowed door to his right, he saw Rachel Brennan lying on a bed, caged in by rails, surrounded by machinery, her eyes closed, a breathing tube taped to her open mouth.

She looked small and wan and irrevocably damaged.

Usually a rock, Cassie's eyes were red and raw and vulnerable, and Jennings was surprised by just how invested she'd become in this case—all because of a simple resemblance to their lost little girl. But he felt it, too, and he marveled at how the mind could so easily trigger such emotions and stir up memories he routinely tried to banish.

But then true grief could never be buried, could it? He was walking proof of that. It merely lurked in the shadows like some hulking beast, waiting to lash out and ravage you mercilessly. Usually when you were the least prepared.

"Where was she found?"

"On the street," Cassie said. "A witness saw her escape from a black SUV and start running, screaming at the top of her lungs. She got about half a block and collapsed. It's a miracle she even got that far."

"And the SUV?"

"It disappeared. No license number, nothing."

Jennings sighed and gestured to Rachel. "I assume Captain Ass Hat knows about this?"

"He still thinks he made the right call. Says considering the part of town she works in, the attack may not even be related to her husband's disappearance."

"Bullshit," Jennings said.

"I think so, too."

"No, I'm saying I *know* it is. I've got proof."

She frowned. "What do you mean?"

Glancing toward the nurse's station, he gestured for her to follow him into the hallway, then pulled out his phone, found Rachel's voicemail, and played it for her.

Cassie's brows went up. "What the hell, Nick? When did you get this?"

A faint jolt of guilt stuttered through him again. "Early this morning. But I didn't know about the message until after you called."

"And where were you when it came in?"

"In bed," he lied. "Asleep."

She eyed him skeptically. "Really? Since when do you sleep after dark?"

"It's been known to happen now and again."

"Or maybe you went to the Bar Vista and wound up sitting down at a table. Maybe when Rachel was getting the crap beat out of her, you were staring at a pair of pocket rockets and wondering how much money you could afford to lose."

He stiffened. "I wasn't playing cards."

"Why don't I believe you?"

"I have no reason to lie."

"But you *are* lying, Nick. I can see it in your eyes. I lived with you long enough and heard enough bullshit to recognize the—"

"I was with a woman, all right?"

This stopped her.

"I heard the ring, but I was occupied and didn't answer. And believe me, I've already considered my share of 'what-ifs' on the drive over here. So don't bust my balls."

Some small part of him wanted her to be upset that he'd been with Anita, but it was obvious she didn't care. What he saw instead was disappointment.

"What the hell was I thinking?" she said. "I should never have gotten you involved in this."

"But you did, didn't you? And now I have no choice but to see it through."

"By doing what?"

"What do you think? Finding out who did this to her."

Cassie shook her head. "No, Nick. That's my job now. Just go home. Go find a game. Be with this woman if she's still on the clock. Do whatever it is you do with your life. This thing has morphed into something new, so Manny and I will handle it. Your services are no longer needed."

Nick had no idea who Manny was, but figured he must be her partner. She'd gone through a lot of them in the last few years.

"So we're back to that? You just shove me aside and pretend I don't exist?"

"This is an active assault investigation now. And I was already crossing the line when I asked for your help. It was a mistake, and I'm sorry. I never should have let Rachel get to me like that. It screwed up my judgment."

"It's still screwing it up. I'm an asset, Cassie, not a liability."

"Really?" she said, her renewed anger sudden and palpable. "Then why is she lying in that room with a tube in her mouth?"

Jennings just stared at her, trying to figure out what was going on inside her head.

Did she really blame *him* for this?

"That's pretty goddamn low, Cass. I don't know what kind of grip this girl has on you, but you've gotta let it go or you'll wind up just like me. I told you last night, she isn't Michelle. She'll never be Michelle. So stop letting her dredge up all this shit inside you."

Cassie looked as if she wanted to slap him, but then the anger subsided and she nodded and closed her eyes, and tears began to roll down her cheeks.

"I can't stop thinking about her, Nick. About Michelle. Wondering why I didn't hear anything that night. Why I didn't wake up."

"Don't," he said. "It wasn't your fault, so don't even go there."

"I can't help it anymore. I've managed to keep this stuff bottled up for years, but now, no matter how I try, I can't seem to let it go." She wiped at her tears. "I miss her, Nick. More than I ever have. I miss her smile, her smell, the sound of her laughter... I've always been the strong one, but look at me. I'm turning into a basket case."

Jennings knew he should respond, but didn't know what to say. It had been a long time since he'd seen her like this. And, as always, his own grief seemed to weigh him down, making it impossible to comfort her, to take her into his arms. So he simply stood there, feeling impotent and ashamed.

Then it was over as quickly as it had started. The confessional was closed.

Cassie sniffed and straightened up and was once again the efficient, no-nonsense cop. The transformation was so abrupt that Jennings thought he might have just witnessed a shift between multiple personalities.

"Sorry," she said. "I shouldn't have done that to you."

"Don't apologize for being human."

"But that's the thing, isn't it? I'm not allowed to be human. I never have been. That was always your territory. When you were falling apart, I was Cassie the Strong. And that's what I need to be now. Otherwise I'll go mad."

"Don't be so hard on yourself."

"Don't worry, I'm not like you, Nick. I'm not a wallower. I may've hit a rough patch, but I'll get past it. I always do." She wiped at her face again and looked at her reflection in a nearby window as if to assess the damage. "I need you to go now, all right? I can't have you interfering in this investigation."

Jennings shook his head. All this drama and they were right back where they'd started.

"I'm sorry, but I can't make that promise."

"You don't have a choice."

"And you don't own me anymore. Neither does the NVPD. If I get in your way, you and your partner will just have to step around me."

Her face hardened, no trace of the distraught Cassie in evidence now.

"If you get in our way," she said, "we'll roll right over you."

11

Anita was still fast asleep when Jennings got back to his apartment, her cute bare ass poking out from beneath the sheets, a reminder of their night together.

He sat on the bed and gently rubbed her back, trying to coax her awake.

It took her a moment, but then she opened her eyes and turned and smiled, and after what he'd just been through with Cassie, it was a welcome sight.

She yawned and stretched. "Just for the record, my expectations weren't too high."

"For what?"

"You don't remember what you told me when I invited myself over? Believe me, hon, you were *not* a disappointment."

"To you, at least."

She frowned. "What does that mean?"

He supposed he could tell her, but his own confessional was closed for the time being. He had work to do.

"Nothing," he said. "Why don't you get up and get dressed and we can talk about Dicky Mars the bartender."

"What about him?"

"I'm hoping you have a way of contacting him, because I want to speak to him as soon as possible."

She hitched herself up on her elbows. "I can give him a call, but I doubt he knows anything about your friend."

"It doesn't hurt to ask."

Dicky Mars was what Jennings would classify as a Vegas old-timer. A big, boisterous man with snow white muttonchops and a handlebar mustache, who would have been at home tending bar at any downtown casino—back when Richard Nixon was still in office.

They met him for coffee at the Over Easy Cafe, an unpretentious, old-style diner housed at the Queen's Landing hotel. As they waited for their order to arrive, Jennings brought out the photograph of Trevor Brennan that he'd taped back together before they left his apartment.

He placed it on the table and slid it across to Mars. "This is my friend Trevor. I've confirmed that two nights ago, at about eleven p.m., he made a call from the pay phone at your club."

Mars nodded, squinted at the photo, then looked at Anita. "I assume you told him how many of the players use that phone on a given night?"

"Oh, I told him."

She had brought a change of clothes to the apartment and was now sporting a crisp white shirt and a pair of blue jeans; her freshly brushed red hair cascaded over her shoulders. Jennings realized she reminded him of that actress, Julianna something, and looked even more beautiful in daylight.

Mars squinted at the photo again, then looked up at him and shook his head. "I hate to disappoint you, son, but he doesn't look familiar. If he made a call from that phone, I didn't see him and probably wouldn't remember him if I had."

The waitress came over and set a cup of coffee in front of each of them, adding a raspberry Danish to Mars's order.

When she was gone, Jennings said, "And you don't know him from the tables?"

Mars took a sip of his coffee. "Trust me, if I did, I'd tell you. I've got nothing to hide. But if he's a player, he isn't a regular. He isn't even a semi-regular."

"Your boss seemed to recognize him. Then tried to pretend he didn't."

"Dimitri? That boy's got just about enough brains to fill a thimble without any spillover. The only reason he has that job is because his uncle owns the place. Fortunately, he only comes in two or three times a week. Any more than that and I'd have to quit."

"How long have you been working at the BVP club?"

"Going on fifteen years," Mars said. "I took the job when the place was still owned by Ace Jackson. And when he turned around and sold it to the goddamn Ruskies, I almost quit right then and there. But that was back during the recession, a bad time to be unemployed. So I stuck it out and never got unstuck." He paused. "I gotta tell you, though, I didn't feel comfortable with the way that deal went down."

"Why's that?"

"Ace loved that club. Put his heart and soul into it. And I never got the feeling he really wanted to sell it. But those Ruskies can be very convincing. It was almost like he was forced into the deal."

"Considering who the buyer was, I wouldn't be surprised."

Mars nodded. "The place has gone downhill since then. Way down hill. And you probably think I'm crazy working for those thugs. Anita too. But the truth is, they pretty much leave us alone and we both need the work. Dimitri stays scarce and the only time we see any of his uncle's men is when..." He paused suddenly and looked at the photograph again.

"What is it?" Jennings asked.

He kept staring at the photo. "I'm thinking I may have jumped the gun a little. Is this picture recent?"

"It was taken two months ago. At Trevor's wedding."

"Wedding?" Mars said, then shook his head. "Then I must be wrong."

"About what?"

"Your friend is pretty clean cut here, but if you trim off about twenty pounds and give him a beard and some scraggly hair... There's something about his eyes that strikes a chord. And I'm thinking he might be one of Koyla's monkeys."

"Who's Kolya?"

"Dimitri's father. Kolya Kozlov. He's second in command to his brother Alexey. Anyway, if you did a little Photoshopping of this face, your friend Trevor would look a lot like one of the meth heads the Kozlovs keep on a leash."

"What do you mean?"

"One of their lackeys. Their gofers. Runs errands, that kind of thing."

"And you've seen him at the club?"

Mars nodded. "If it's the same guy, yeah. He comes in a couple nights a week to pick up and drop off packages. Sometimes Kolya's with him, but most of the time he's alone."

"What sort of packages?"

"Son, if I knew that, I probably wouldn't be long for this world. It's none of my business and I don't intend to get curious." He slid the photo over to Anita. "Take a look at the eyes. Doesn't that look like Govnyuk?"

"Govnyuk?" Jennings said.

"That's what Kolya calls him. Govnyuk do this. Govnyuk do that. At first I thought it was his given name, but Dimitri once told me it's Russian for 'worm'. Or 'nobody'."

Anita was staring intently at the photo now. "You know, now that you mention it, the eyes do look familiar. But if this is him, he's been through one heck of a transformation in a very short time."

"Welcome to the world of meth," Mars said. "I don't know where Alexy and his brother find these guys, but word around the water cooler is that they treat 'em like dirt. Not that that's much different than most of the people they interact with."

"There's more than one of these errand boys?"

Mars took a bite of his danish. "They come and go. And most of them look in dire need of rehab. The way I've heard it, they find themselves in debt to Alexey and he makes them work it off in indentured servitude. He gets some kind of kick out of humiliating the hell out of 'em."

"You've gotta be kidding me."

"I didn't believe it at first, either. But looking at some of these guys, especially guys like Govnyuk, and you start to think it *is* true and that the Kozlov brothers are sadistic bastards."

Jennings tried, but couldn't quite wrap his head around the idea. Was it possible that Trevor Brennan had somehow fallen prey to these men? Had he racked up such a large gambling debt that the only way to work it off was to essentially become the Kozlovs' slave?

The idea was crazy. Maybe just crazy enough to be true.

But why the meth? Had that been part of what fueled Trevor's gambling addiction and his need for cash, or had it come later, after he'd fallen into the hands of Alexey and Kolya—assuming he had.

Jennings turned to Anita. "Are you buying any of this?"

"I've heard some of the rumors, too, but no, I never believed them. Maybe I just didn't want to."

Neither did Jennings. But the world was full of people who had done far worse. The depths of human depravity seemed to have no limits. There were parents who drowned their children or locked their daughters in basements for years on end. Priests who preyed on young boys in the houses of God. Men who snatched little girls from their beds at night and dumped them in ditches when they were done abusing them.

"Where do I find the Kozlovs?" he asked Mars.

"They've got a big old house in Seven Hills."

Jennings whistled. Seven Hills was a gated community with real estate values that easily topped a million and didn't stop there.

"But don't let that fool you," Mars continued. "These are not people you want to be butting heads with."

"They may have put a young woman in the hospital last night and I'm not about to let that stand. What about Dimitri? Where do I find him when he isn't at the club?"

Anita put a hand on his forearm. "Nick, are you sure you want to do this?"

"Do what? I just want to ask a few questions."

"You saw how Dimitri is. He's not a man you want to piss off. And if the rumors are true, Alexey and Kolya are even worse."

"I appreciate the concern, but I'm not exactly an amateur. I spent a lot of years dealing with the worst this world has to offer, so I'm pretty sure I can handle myself."

Anita and Mars exchanged a look, as if to say, *who does he think he's kidding*?

"Don't worry," Jennings said. "None of this will blow back on either of you."

Anita squeezed his arm. "That's not what I'm worried about. I don't want you getting yourself killed before we've had a chance to have a second date."

Jennings couldn't help himself. He smiled.

This woman had a way of making that happen and he wasn't sure why.

But he liked it.

"I'll keep that in mind," he said. "Now tell me where I can find Dimitri."

12

When you want to confront someone who's twice your size and mean as a snake yet avoid getting your head bashed in, it's probably not a good idea to ring the front doorbell.

Fortunately, since leaving the force, Jennings had developed a few skills that would give him other options. The danger, of course, was breaking into a man's apartment in broad daylight. But Jennings figured the benefits outweighed the risk, and decided to take the chance that Dimitri Koslov's neighbors wouldn't notice—or care—that a guy was climbing into a second story window.

He was also taking the chance that Dimitri was a night owl and would still be fast asleep this late in the morning. Jennings knew there were all kinds of things that could go wrong with this scenario—and that this could well be a dead end, or even a *deadly* one—but what the hell. He'd always been reckless so why break the pattern now?

Dimitri Kozlov's apartment was one of four units in a small building just north of Fremont, a second story walk-up in a neighborhood where break-ins were a part of everyday life. Several of the windows in the area had bars on them, but Jennings had lucked out with Dimitri's unit on two counts:

1. No bars or other deterrents in place; and

2. An adjoining carport structure with a roof that just happened to give him easier access to Dimitri's bathroom window.

Whoever had designed this hodgepodge of a dwelling had not been particularly security conscious. But as Jennings had learned —thanks to his extracurricular activities with Scully—security was far too often an afterthought.

Before making the jaunt to chez Dimitri, he had taken Anita back to his apartment to get her things and to retrieve the Glock 19 and hip holster from the lock box on a shelf in his bedroom closet. It was his old LVMPD service weapon that he rarely had use for, but he figured that since he was about to confront a giant, it wouldn't hurt to arm himself.

Anita had tried again to convince him not to mess with the Koslovs, but he kept thinking about that girl lying in a coma at the

ICU, and knew he had no choice. If Dicky Mars had been right about the guy he knew as Govnyuk, and the Koslovs were holding Trevor Brennan against his will, chances were good they had something to do with Rachel's assault.

If so, Jennings would have to make sure they understood the error of their ways.

When he dropped Anita off at her apartment, she leaned toward him and pecked his cheek. "I still want that second date."

"Why on earth would you want to get involved with a loser like me?"

She smiled. "Because I like you, Nick. Isn't that enough?"

"I'm not used to being liked."

"I'll *help* you get used to it. Assuming Dimitri doesn't snap you in two."

"He'll have to get hold of me first."

Now, as Jennings stood outside Dimitri's apartment negotiating the climb to the top of the adjoining carport, he thought about how Anita had made him feel this morning.

Wanted.

He wasn't used to that, either.

And maybe it didn't matter that the one person *he* wanted would never be able to reach across that yawning divide separating them. Maybe it was time to let go of the old dream and create something new.

If that was even possible for a guy like him.

Jennings had always been something of a natural athlete, and the climb to the carport rooftop was easy, even with a crowbar in hand. He wasted no time crossing to Dimitri's bathroom window, took a quick look around for prying eyes, then jammed the business end of the crowbar beneath the sill and jimmied the window open.

It didn't offer much resistance—or make much noise—and within seconds he was climbing into a small, dank bathroom that smelled of mold, urine and aftershave.

He heard the sound of snoring coming from what he assumed was a bedroom, which meant that Dimitri Kozlov was fast asleep as predicted. He sent a small prayer of thanks to whoever was up there listening.

So far, so good.

Bringing out his cuffs—also retrieved from his closet—he left the bathroom and followed the sound until he was standing in Dimitri's bedroom. The giant was draped across a mattress that was too small for his massive body, his mouth agape, his eyelids twitching as if he were deep in a dream state.

One of his arms dangled over the side of the bed and Jennings knew his luck was holding.

Approaching him carefully, Jennings crouched down, quietly slipped one cuff over the metal bed frame, then clicked it shut, glancing up at Dimitri's face for signs that he'd awakened.

A loud, lusty snore put an end to that fear.

This next part would be the trickiest, but judging by the depth of Dimitri's sleep, Jennings doubted he had much to worry about. Still, he moved slowly and cautiously as he placed the other cuff around the dangling wrist, then clicked it shut.

This time the sound—or sensation—caused a disturbance in the force. Dimitri snorted and briefly opened his eyes before closing them again and falling back asleep. Judging by the beer bottles and assortment of pills littering the night stand, the Russian was a heavy user, which had no doubt contributed to his current state.

Rising to his feet, Jennings checked the bottles for one that still had liquid in it, found one half full, and lifted it from the nightstand. He then pulled his Glock from its holster with his free hand, turned toward Dimitri and held the bottle above his head.

Bracing himself, he poured the remaining beer into the sleeping giant's face.

Dimitri's eyes flew open and he jerked awake sputtering and cursing in both English and Russian. The moment he saw Jennings, he tried to launch himself off the bed, only to discover he was cuffed to the frame.

He roared in anger and jerked at the cuffs.

Jennings aimed the Glock right between his eyes. "Shut the hell up."

The sight of the gun barrel was a bracing slap to the face. Dimitri immediately calmed himself, but when he looked up at Jennings he was still simmering with rage. "You are dead man."

"I don't think you're in any position to be making threats, asshole. It's a good thing I don't scare easily."

Dimitri's eyes narrowed. "You are not police."

"Not anymore, no."

"Then what you want from me?"

Jennings tossed the empty bottle to the floor, then pulled out the taped photograph of Trevor Brennan and showed it to him. "I'm here to give you another look at my friend's face. And this time, when I ask if you know him, I want the truth."

"I say truth last night."

"Really? Then why didn't you tell me about Guvnyuk?"

The giant's expression gave him away, but he tried anyway. "Guvnyuk? Who is Guvnyuk?"

"Don't ever go into acting, Dimitri. You know as well as I do that that's the nickname your father and uncle gave their little errand boy. An errand boy who just happens to look a lot like the man in this picture."

"No," Dimitri said. "Not possible. Why they care about this man?"

"That's the million dollar question, isn't it? One I expect you to answer."

Dimitri said nothing. Just stared at him with that barely contained rage.

"You seem to be forgetting I've got a gun pointed at your head, and trust me, you wouldn't be the first douche bag I've shot. I'm not the most patient guy in the world."

Dimitri seemed to be considering this as he stared into the barrel of the Glock. Finally, he caved. "He not just errand boy. He is fighter."

"Fighter? What does that mean?"

"He come to private game and lose many, many dollars. Then he ask Uncle Alexey for borrow and promise he good for payback. But he lie. He don't have money. He never have money. So Uncle Alexey punish him. Make him work."

"As a fighter?"

"He good with fists. So uncle recruit him for Bitva Noch."

"What the hell is that?"

"Bitva Noch," he repeated, then struggled to find the

translation. "Battle Night."

Jennings wasn't quite sure he understood. "You mean boxing?"

"Boxing for pussy. This is fight. Real fight. No glove. No rule. Last man standing is winner."

"And the loser? What happens to him?"

Dimitri said nothing, but Jennings wasn't stupid. The Koslovs were running an underground fight club. Human pit bulls unleashed against each other until one of them was either crippled or dead. And the man no longer standing would undoubtedly be carted away and planted somewhere in the desert. Maybe it wasn't Trevor Brennan's bones the coyotes were gnawing on—not yet, at least—but there were bones nonetheless.

Jennings imagined that such an enterprise could be quite lucrative to the Koslovs. The spectators were bound to be filthy rich—to keep the club exclusive—and a percentage would be taken off the top of each bet they made. He remembered a slew of arrests several years ago in Los Angeles, when a gang of "entrepreneurs" was found to be recruiting homeless men for a series of increasingly brutal street fights. When asked how he could exploit the men this way, the leader of the gang had said, "They're a bunch of drunks. What else are they good for?"

From a criminal's perspective, running a fight club was no different than running an unauthorized brothel or a trafficking in drugs. Just another Sin City profiteering scheme, geared toward gamblers who liked to get their kicks off the beaten path, by people with no regard for human life.

But that was pretty much the way of the world these days, wasn't it?

"What's your role in all of this?" he asked Dimitri.

"I manage poker club. What my father and his brother do is not my business."

"Yet you seem to know all about it."

Dimitri shrugged. "They are family. I hear things."

"And what about the girl? What did you hear about her?"

The low-slung brow furrowed. "What girl?"

"The girl Govnyuk called last night. Just like he did the night before, from your club. The girl someone nearly beat to death."

"I know nothing of girl."

"My finger really wants to pull this trigger," Jennings warned.

"I know nothing of girl!" Dimitri shouted, and almost made Jennings a believer.

"You lie, you die," Jennings said. "Remember that."

He was about to mention the phone calls Dimitri had made after Jennings had left the club last night. But then he thought better of it. Tipping what he knew might put Anita in danger.

"I do not lie," Dimitri said, his bloodshot eyes flicking from the gun to Nick's face. "I tell you truth. I answer question. Now you let me go."

"When is the next fight?"

"They fight most nights. Never Sunday."

"So there's one tonight?"

"Yes. Tonight."

"What time and where?"

Dimitri's rage began to rise again. "Why you care? You be dead by then."

"We've all gotta go sometime."

13

Being a native of Vegas and a former cop, Jennings was well aware of what neighborhoods the average tourist would be wise to avoid at night.

One of those was North 28th Street near Bonanza Road.

A few years back, 28th and B had been deemed the fourth most dangerous neighborhood in America. Jennings didn't know how accurate that statistic was, but in his days on the force he'd had more than one deadly encounter in the area and didn't relish the idea of going there alone.

Still, at 10:30 p.m., he pulled his Vic into the parking lot of what was once a thriving Catholic church nestled between a fenced in vacant lot and a rundown apartment building. The church had been abandoned and left to rot for a good twenty years, but its parking lot, which was hidden from the street at the end of a long drive, was crowded with cars—most of them considerably more upscale than the Vic.

So Dimitri hadn't lied. This was the latest home of Bitva Noch', the Koslov fight club. Place your bets, ladies and gentlemen. Watch a man be brutally beaten to death in a house of God.

After getting the information he needed from Dimitri, Jennings had found himself in a bit of a bind. He wasn't about to shoot the guy—although the thought had crossed his mind—but he couldn't very well leave him there to hop on his phone and make a flurry of calls to his father and uncle.

Fortunately, Jennings had thought ahead, and the pharmacy on Dimitri's nightstand allowed him to improvise. He had intended to hit the big guy a few times, hoping to knock him out, but a couple of Ambien did the trick instead, and made things a lot less messy. Jennings forced him at gunpoint to take the pills, and waited until Dimitri had drifted into a harmless stupor. Then he carefully removed the cuffs, got on Dimitri's land line, and called 911.

They picked up on the second ring. "Nine-one-one operator, what is your emergency?"

"I've got a man here, I think he may have O.D.'d. He's about to pass out and isn't breathing too well."

The operator asked for details and Jennings told her he was a neighbor who had heard a crash and found the door unlocked. He gave her a phony name and Dimitri's address and she said an ambulance and police unit were on their way.

After he hung up, he reached into his pocket and pulled out a nickel bag of heroin and a dope kit he had scored from one of Scully's friends, then made sure they were clearly visible on the nightstand. Then he knocked over the nightstand lamp and let himself out through the front door.

Jennings had waited in his Vic until the ambulance and police cruiser arrived, and watched as the paramedics brought Dimitri out on a gurney and struggled to get him down the steps to the first floor. The two patrol officers emerged from the apartment a moment later, and as one carried a couple of evidence bags down to his cruiser, the other knocked on the door of Dimitri's neighbor.

Things were bound to get a bit confusing in the next several minutes, but the giant would either wake up in the hospital or in LVMPD lock-up, and would have a lot of explaining to do. Whatever the case, he'd be out of commission for quite some time.

Now, as Jennings pulled into the abandoned church's parking lot and parked next to a white Mercedes, he thought about what he'd done, and couldn't muster up even a sliver of guilt. As a cop, he had never once set up a perp, even when the temptation was strong, but things were different now, and sometimes you did what had to be done.

Another lesson he'd learned from Scully.

The bouncer who opened the rear door of the church was nearly as big as Dimitri Koslov, and twice as ugly.

He looked Jennings up and down, and said in a thick accent, "Something I do for you?"

"Babochka," Jennings said, giving him the Russian word for butterfly—which he thought might be a reference to Mohammed Ali. He hoped it was the correct password, because the wrong one would likely cause him serious trouble, and he wondered for a moment if Dimitri had set him up. But then Dimitri didn't strike him as the kind of guy who was capable of setting *anyone* up.

To his relief, the bouncer gave him a crooked grin and nodded.

"Welcome to Bitva Noch." Then he opened the door wide and waited for Jennings to step inside.

The exterior of the church was little more than a box and steeple built of crumbling slate, but a row of work lights inside revealed that the interior truly reflected its state of disrepair. Dilapidated and broken down pews, an altar that was stripped bare, cracked stained glass windows, several of which had been boarded over with plywood. The place felt as if the good guys had lost and it was now inhabited by evil—which probably wasn't too far from the truth.

After closing the door, the bouncer gestured for Jennings to put his hands on a nearby wall, then gave him a pat down for weapons. He found Jennings's cell phone and pocketed it, saying, "You get back after." Then, satisfied that Jennings was clean, indicated a set of steps to the left of the altar that led down to a lower floor. "Fight start in thirty minutes. Bet big, win big."

"I'll keep that in mind," Jennings said, then crossed to the steps and headed down.

A moment later he was standing in a dim basement, more work lights placed in a circle, illuminating the center of the room. There were a hundred or more people milling about, drinking booze from plastic cups, their faces alight with anticipation. The crowd was a good mix of men and women, most of them white, and most wearing expensive clothes and shoes and jewelry and sporting thousand dollar haircuts that told the world they had money. Lots of money. People who were used to getting what they wanted, when they wanted it, and making sure everyone damn well knew it.

Jennings had worn his best suit in hopes of blending in, but knew he didn't have the attitude of superiority to make it work. He hoped no one would notice, but within seconds of wading into the crowd, he felt eyes on him and turned.

Across the room, near a small makeshift bar, a Hispanic man in his mid-forties stood watching him, but averted his gaze the moment Jennings made eye contact. The guy was dressed to the nines, looking very stylish in a tailor made suit, but Jennings didn't like the vibe he was giving off.

Had he just been made by one of the Kozlovs' men? The guy

certainly didn't look the type—whatever that was.

A moment later the man shifted his gaze again and smiled at an approaching blonde in a form fitting dress and enough jewelry to break a small bank. They kissed and then turned away from Jennings as if he didn't exist.

False alarm?

Apparently so. But Jennings still didn't feel good about the guy.

Off to the left was an oblong table, manned by three attractive women who were taking bets from the spectators. The lines were fairly long and the bets large (judging by the amount of cash changing hands), and the Kozlovs were no doubt taking a nice cut of each one of them.

Jennings worked his way through the crowd toward the betting table, and saw a hallway beyond it. There were a couple of Slavic thugs milling around nearby and he figured the Koslovs and their fighters must be back there somewhere, prepping for the night's entertainment.

After a moment, a young couple emerged from the hallway, and Jennings thought he knew what else was back there. Moving around the table, he headed that way and was stopped by one of the thugs.

"Toilet?" he asked.

The thug looked him over, then gestured. "End of hall, turn left."

Jennings thanked him and headed down a narrow corridor until he found an adjoining hallway and turned left. A door hung open at the end of this new hallway and he saw a toilet and sink inside. He moved to it and turned as he closed the door, getting a look at the opposite end.

What he saw was another open door, a lit room beyond, and a man inside, speaking heatedly on his cell phone. Jennings recognized his face from an Internet search that had netted him a large number of photographs.

Alexey Koslov.

But then another man crossed Jennings's view, wearing a pair of jeans and no shirt—a thin but muscular young man with stringy, unwashed hair and the nervous energy of a meth addict.

Jennings froze in place, sensing he had just hit pay dirt. Though he had never met the man, he knew instinctively who he was.

Trevor Brennan.

14

Brennan crossed the hall to another doorway, looking like a man who had been trapped in hell for a very long time, his eyes sunken, and sores beginning to form on his right cheek and forehead.

Jennings now understood why it had taken Dicky Mars and Anita so long to recognize him in the photograph. He barely looked like the same guy.

The only thing that remained was a large, muscular physique, though it was beginning to show signs of wear and tear. He could see how the guy might be formidable in a fight—especially with the meth fueling him—and suspected that was why he was still alive.

Sooner or later, however, the drug would take its toll—if it hadn't done too much damage already—and Jennings didn't doubt that the Kozlovs were supplying it to him to keep their fighter in line for as long as he was a viable moneymaker.

And when he no longer was, they'd discard him like an empty bottle of vodka.

Brennan opened the door and disappeared behind it. As it closed, Jennings emerged from the restroom. Keeping his eyes on Alexey Kozlov, who was still in the midst of his heated phone call, he crossed to the door and quickly let himself inside.

He came upon another short hallway and to the left was an open doorway. He stepped through it into what had once been a small lunch or break room, with three dingy tables and some metal folding chairs. A wan overhead light did its best to illuminate the place, but the effect was like a broken man's nightmare.

Brennan sat hunched on one of the folding chairs, meth pipe in hand, lighter poised.

He looked up sharply at Jennings. "Who the fuck are you?"

Jennings raised his hands. "Relax, Trevor. I'm a friend of Rachel's."

Brennan seemed both confused and surprised by this. "...What?"

"She sent me to find you. To take you back home to her."

Brennan shook his head. "No, no, that can't be right. I just saw Rachel last night."

"Oh? And where was this?"

He squinted, as if trying to capture the memory. "...I think it was last night. I called her and asked her to come help me... to help me pay Alexey and Kolya the money I owe them, so they'd let me go."

"And how did that work out?"

Brennan suddenly turned back to his task, raising the lighter again and thumbing it alive. "I don't want to talk about it."

He took a deep draw, the smell of burning chemicals filling the room. Jennings walked over, grabbed the pipe out of his hand and threw it against a wall. It bounced to the floor in pieces.

"What the hell did you do that for?" Brennan snarled as he rose to retrieve it. But Jennings planted a hand on his chest and sat him back down.

"I think you already know this, Trevor, but I'll tell you how it worked out with Rachel. Right now she's in the ICU at Carson County General fighting for her life. Somebody beat the shit out of her. Do you remember that part?"

Trevor frowned. "You better not be touching me like that again, mister. Who the hell are you, anyway?"

"Forget who I am. Tell me what happened to Rachel."

He started to get up again. "I don't know what hap—"

"Bullshit." Jennings pushed him back down.

Brennan scowled. "You keep doing that and I might have to tune you up a bit."

"In your condition, I'm surprised you can light that pipe. Will your opponent be in the same condition? Is that part of the show? Dueling crank heads? Extra hits between rounds?"

"Fuck you."

"How long have they been feeding you the Okie coke, Trevor? Or did you have the habit before you ran into the Koslovs?"

"No fucking way," Brennan said, shaking his head vigorously. "It's what they do, man. It's how they get you."

"How much money did you lose to them?"

"What difference does it make, I'll never be able to pay it."

"How much?"

"About three hundred grand after all the interest."

Jennings nodded. "So you called Rachel and asked her to help you pay it off and what happened? Did she refuse?"

"No," Brennan said. "She loves me. She just wanted me to come home. Said she'd pay anything they want."

"So what went wrong?"

Brennan stared forlornly at the broken pipe on the floor. "Just let me take one hit and I'll—"

"Tell me," Jennings insisted. "Now."

Brennan visited the memory again in his mind, a look of pure agony on his face.

"When she showed up at his place, Alexey went ballistic. Started screaming at me, said I should be ashamed of myself, begging some little piece of pussy to pay my debts. What kind of man am I? He wasn't interested in her money. Not one bit. Because that's the game he plays, man. It's how he gets his kicks. He wants to control you. To grind you down with drugs and abuse and make you feel like a worthless dog, which is exactly what I am." He looked at the pipe again. "He told me I needed to learn a lesson in obedience and Rachel was part of it."

"So he beat her. Is that it?"

"No. He'd never get his hands dirty like that."

"Then who? His brother? One of his thugs?"

"No, man, no. You don't understand what he's like. When he teaches you a lesson he really teaches it to you."

"What the hell does that mean?"

Brennan's eyes were blazing now. "Don't you fucking get it, asshole? *I'm* the one who beat her. Me. With my own goddamn hands. Alexey said that was the only way I could make it up to him."

Jennings stared at him in complete disbelief, wondering how anyone could have such a hold on a man that he'd beat his own wife into a coma. Wondering what kind of man would want to *have* that kind of hold.

A sadist. Or a sociopath.

He saw Brennan's shame and discomfort and Brennan looked away, his gaze again drifting toward the broken pipe on the floor. And in a way it symbolized everything that Brennan had become.

He hung his head, and in a move the mirrored his comatose wife, stared at his fidgeting hands.

"Why'd you have to do that, man? I didn't do anything to you."

Before Jennings could respond, the door in the hallway slammed open and two thugs the size of cargo ships burst into the room behind them. Jennings wheeled around, but it was too late.

One of the thugs let loose a blast of a Taser gun, the darts slamming into Jennings's chest.

He went down hard, a white, burning pain coursing through his body, completely immobilizing him. Then a boot kicked him in the side of the head...

...and everything went black.

15

When he awoke he was tied to a chair.

His chest hurt and his head pounded like a bitch.

He heard the muffled sound of cheers and gathered enough brain energy to remember where he was. The fight must have started. Trevor Brennan was facing off against whatever poor soul had been chosen to challenge him.

Then he realized that the sound wasn't coming from another room, but from a nearby TV, parked in front of a large desk.

Behind that desk was Alexey Kozlov, smiling benevolently as he watched a screen Jennings couldn't see.

Then he shifted his gaze to his guest, his accent Russian, his English flawless. "Welcome back, Mr. Jennings. I hope you do not mind that I took the liberty of checking your wallet to find out who you are. Guvnyuk did not know your name."

Jennings swiveled his head and saw Trevor Brennan sitting on a chair in the corner, staring at his hands. He was much calmer now, and it was clear he had gotten that second hit of crank he'd so desperately wanted.

Kozlov showed Jennings one of his old business cards. "I see you used to be with the metropolitan police. Very impressive the way you scratched out the phone number and rewrote it. You are retired?"

"Does it matter?"

"Oh, very much so. I would not want to keep an officer of the law from doing the work the citizens of Las Vegas hired him to do. On the other hand, if that officer is no longer official, you can understand why I might have concerns about him coming to my place of business to harass my employees."

"Employees?"

"Guvnyuk is working off a debt to me. But I am sure you already know that."

"He has a name," Jennings said. "A real one."

Kozlov smiled. "Yes, of course, but what are names? I prefer Guvnyuk. Much more fitting, no?"

"No," Jennings said.

Kozlov shrugged. "A small point of contention. Guvnyuk tells me his young wife asked you to find him and bring him home. But, as you know, that situation has already been resolved."

"Is that what you call it?" Jennings said. "The girl is in a coma."

"A travesty, yes, but you must understand that she was part of a very important lesson in loyalty." He gestured. "Guvnyuk, bring Mr. Jennings around here so that he may enjoy the show."

Brennan nodded and got to his feet. He moved around behind Jennings's chair and tilted it backwards, dragging it by its hind legs across the cement floor.

"Good boy," Kozlov said, as if speaking to a pet. "You see, Mr. Jennings, many years ago, when I was still with the KGB, I became interested in the art of coercive persuasion. I am quite proud of my ability to break a man down and watch him come to the realization that his mind is not his own. It is very rewarding."

"Sure," Jennings said. "If you're a sadist."

Brennan continued dragging him, pulling him around so that the TV screen was in view.

"But you see," Kozlov continued, "there is never a guarantee that you will be one hundred percent successful. As in our young friend's case, when he attempted to call his bride. That was a violation of his training that could not be ignored. So I told him to call her again."

Facing the screen now, Jennings saw a video—shot in the church basement—of several of Kozlov's thugs clapping and cheering. In the center of the room was Trevor Brennan, mercilessly beating Rachel.

Jennings closed his eyes. "You sick son of a bitch."

"Keep in mind, I did not know about Guvnyuk's transgression until someone who claimed to be a police officer came into my poker club and showed his photograph to my nephew Dimitri. I assume that was you?"

"You already know it was."

Kozlov spread his hands. "So, in effect, you are to blame for this young girl's distress."

"Fuck you," Jennings said.

"Yes, indeed. Fuck me. But let us not forget which of us is sitting behind this desk and which is tied to a chair. You are about to learn a lesson in control, Mr. Jennings, and what it means to lose

it. Before we get started, however, I am told that Guvnyuk's opponent has finally arrived, and there are a lot of paying customers
who are anxious to see them fight. Is that not right, Guvnyuk?"

"That's right, Mr. Kozlov."

"And are you ready to prove your loyalty to me?"

"Yes, Mr. Kozlov."

Kozlov looked at Jennings. "You see, he understands that he has
become a liability, and has agreed to pay off his debt by taking
what you Americans call a dive tonight. Many of our guests will be
betting on him to win, but I am afraid they are about to be sorely
disappointed. And depending on the mercy of his opponent—and
the crowd, of course—this could well be the last time you see
him." He smiled. "But not to worry, you will be seeing plenty of me
from here on out. Before the week is over you will be wanting to
prove your loyalty to me just as Guvnyuk has."

"Don't count on it," Jennings said.

"Oh, but I do, Mr. Jennings, I do. The human psyche is a fragile
thing and I so enjoy exploiting it. One of life's great pleasures." He
snapped his fingers at Brennan. "Give him his medicine, will you?"

Brennan nodded, crossed to Kozlov's desk and opened a
drawer, taking out a small syringe full of liquid.

"What our young friend has in his hand," Kozlov said, "is a dose
of pure methamphetamine. I do not know if you have had any
personal experience with the drug, but I am certain during your
time as politsiya you must have seen its effects. It travels straight
to the central nervous system and produces a high so intense that
it is not unusual for someone to become addicted after a single
dose."

"Sounds lovely."

"Oh it is. You will be awake for days. And in that time we will
get to know each other, you and I." He smiled. "Perhaps together
we can come up with a name for you. Something suitable." He
gestured. "Give the man his shot, Guvnyuk."

Brennan nodded and moved around the desk to Jennings,
prepping the syringe for injection. Jennings stared at the dripping
needle, his heart pounding. "You don't want to do this, Trevor. It's
not who you are."

Kozlov laughed. "I *made* him who he is, Mr. Jennings. How

could you have forgotten that so quickly?"

Brennan moved closer.

"Look at the TV screen," Jennings said to him. "Look what you're doing to the woman you love. She's in a hospital right now, fighting for her life, because of him. Because of what he made you do."

Kozlov waved a hand at them. "You know that was necessary for your training, Guvnyuk. Now administer the shot."

Standing in front of Jennings now, Brennan untied one of Jennings's arms and twisted it to expose the inner elbow. Jennings suddenly jerked in his chair, trying to move away.

Kozlov sighed. "Please, my friend. There is no point in fighting the inevitable."

Jennings kept jerking. "Is it inevitable, Trevor? What you've become? Or are you in there somewhere, remembering what he's done to you? And what he made you do to Rachel. Look at that TV screen, Trevor. Look at what he made you do."

Brennan glanced only briefly at the screen, but went back to his task. Grabbing Jennings by the neck, he held him in place, and Jennings tried to move, but was paralyzed by Brennan's grasp. His heart slamming against his chest, he steeled himself for the sting of the needle...

"Don't... do... this..." he managed to croak. "Think about... Rachel..."

And just as Brennan was about to drive the needle home, something shifted in his gaze. A trace of life appeared behind his eyes. He once again glanced at the horror on the TV screen, then let out a roar so loud and so primal it made Jennings's chest ache.

Brennan let him go and wrenched the needle down hard, stabbing it into his own thigh.

Kozlov's eyes went wide and he jumped to his feet. "You fucking idiot!"

But now, as Jennings watched, the drug took hold and Brennan suddenly transformed from obedient slave to enraged crank head. He turned on Kozlov and lunged toward him across the desk just as Kozlov pulled a pistol from his drawer and started firing.

One shot went wild, but two slugs hit Brennan in the chest. He kept moving as if they were nothing more than bug bites. Roaring in wild, animal rage, he grabbed Kozlov by the neck, yanked him out from behind the desk, and threw him to the floor.

Then he started to pound on Kozlov, blow after blow after blow, the Russian's face turning to a bloody pulp before Jennings's eyes.

When he was done, Brennan stood over the body, breathing hard, blood running from his knuckles and the holes in his chest, tears streaming down his face. "I... loved... her..."

Then he collapsed to the floor.

16

A split-second after Brennan hit the floor, the door burst open.

Jennings had expected the room to fill with Kozlov's thugs, but was surprised instead to see the Hispanic man who'd been eyeing him earlier in the fight room. His blonde girlfriend was at his side, both sporting hardware and ready to use it. How they'd gotten the weapons past the bouncer was anyone's guess, but Jennings suspected the blonde had done the smuggling.

They rushed into the room and stopped short when they saw the two bodies on the floor.

"Jesus H. Christ," the Hispanic man said.

Jennings heard shouts and squeals coming from the other room and the unmistakable sounds of a raid taking place. The police were here and he had no doubt that the Hispanic man and the blonde had been working undercover.

"They had a bit of a disagreement," Jennings told them.

The blonde snorted. "No shit. Is that Alexey Kozlov himself?"

"It *was*," Jennings said.

The Hispanic man moved to the chair and began untying him. "You're Nick Jennings, right? I made you the moment you showed up."

"Do we know each other?"

"Manny Rodriguez. I'm Cassie's partner."

Jennings rubbed his wrists. "No kidding. Is she here?"

"She is. And the minute she sees you, she is *not* gonna be happy."

Jennings shrugged. "Story of my life, friend. Story of my life."

Cassie was indeed pissed.

"I should throw you in the tank along with the rest of them," she said. "Didn't I tell you to go home and forget about this?"

They were standing in the church parking lot full of squad cars, where a phalanx of uniformed officers were busy corralling Kozlov's thugs and several of his guests.

"Like that was gonna happen," Jennings said. "How did you guys wind up here, anyway?"

"I could ask you the same question."

He shrugged. "Just blind luck."

"Uh-huh. We went to the Bar Vista Poker Club to question Dimitri Kozlov and found out he'd managed to get himself arrested this afternoon. Imagine that. And when we paid him a visit in lock up, he decided he'd rather trade information than spend the next few years in jail on a drug beef."

"I guess he's not as stupid as I thought he was."

"He also claims some guy broke into his apartment, threatened him and set him up with a bag of heroin. You wouldn't know anything about that, would you?"

"Not a clue. Wish I'd thought of it though."

She looked at him and sighed. "I don't know why I even bother."

Fortunately for the police, the Kozlov brothers had videotaped a number of their fight club activities, which, along with the video of Trevor beating his wife, had given them more than enough evidence to make a number of arrests, including Alexey Kozlov's gang and several of the attendees.

The only one missing was Kolya Kozlov, brother to Alexey and father to Dimitri.

It later came to light that Kolya had been in New York on business during the night in question, and when he got word of his brother's death and the subsequent arrests, had hightailed it out of the country, reportedly catching Skyway Flight 12 to Rome, of all places.

He hasn't been seen nor heard from since.

Two weeks later, Jennings stood on the sidewalk and watched Rachel Brennan walk out of Clark County General on crutches.

It was a miracle she could walk at all.

A bigger miracle that she was alive.

He'd gone to pick her up, hoping to talk to her, to console her for her loss.

But the moment she saw him, she turned away and hailed a cab instead.

He supposed he couldn't blame her. She needed someone to take the face of the bad guy in all of this. He still wasn't so sure that ignoring his ringing phone the night he was with Anita didn't make him one.

He didn't try to stop her. Just watched her climb painfully inside the cab, her battered but mending face still showing traces of Michelle.

His heart ached at the sight of her–and at the memory of his little girl lost.

Then again, his heart often ached.

It probably always would.

When she was gone, he sat in his car for a long moment, thinking about hunting down a game, but thinking, too, that maybe he needed a little therapy. The kind that Anita Kool was so good at.

His mind made up, he pulled out his phone and gave her a call.

ALSO BY
ROBERT GREGORY BROWNE

TRIAL JUNKIES SERIES

Trial Junkies
Trial Junkies 2: Negligence
Trial Junkies 3: No Paradise
(coming soon)

FOURTH DIMENSION THRILLERS

Kiss Her Goodbye
Whisper in the Dark
Kill Her Again

ALEXANDRA POE SERIES
(co-written with Brett Battles)

Poe
Takedown

NICK JENNINGS THRILLERS

Bottom Deal
Side Steal

STANDALONE THRILLERS

The Innocent Ones
The Paradise Prophecy

9 781979 559881